Wines and Spirits

LOOKING BEHIND THE LABEL

Wines and Spirits

LOOKING BEHIND THE LABEL

Produced and published by the
Wine & Spirit Education Trust

with a foreword by
The Master Vintner

Wine & Spirit Education Trust
39-45 Bermondsey Street, London SE1 3XF
e-mail wset@wset.co.uk
internet www.wsetglobal.com

A CIP catalogue record for this book is available from the British Library

ISBN 978 0 951793 68 8

PHOTOGRAPHIC CREDITS
CEPHAS: 13, 32, 53 (Kevin Judd), 33 (Nigel Blythe), 60 (Andy
Christodolo), 63 (Karine Bossavy), 64, 45, 48, 59 (Mick Rock),

10, 36, 27 (Sopexa); 12, 52 (Wines of South Africa); 27 (CIVB); 50
(ICEX, Spanish Institute for Foreign Trade); 51, 68 (ICEP Portugal)

WSET: 6, 7, 74, 76 (WSET collection); 14, 23 (Nicolla Greaves); 19, 41,
47, 54, 56, 57, 67, 71, 73 (Michael Buriak); 72 (Erica Dent),

COVER PICTURES
Background picture: Victoria Clare
Top and middle: Nicolla Greaves
Bottom: Erica Dent

LABELS
Labels supplied by Direct Wines Ltd, with many thanks to
Martin Campion

MAPS
Maps designed by Chris Groom, Design Study

Designed by Peter Dolton
Production services by Book Production Consultants Ltd
Printed and bound in Italy by Studio Fasoli, Verona

Contents

SECTION 4: OTHER STYLES OF WINE

SECTION 5: SPIRITS AND LIQUEURS

APPENDICES

Foreword

The Vintners' Company, with its first Charter in 1363, which allowed a monopoly of trade in wine with Gascony, is one of the Twelve Great Livery Companies of the City of London. With its origins in the middle ages, the Company has strong and unbroken links with the wine trade and some 40% of its members are currently in the trade.

In 1953, the Vintners's Company founded the Institute of Masters of Wine and in 1969, in conjunction with the Wine and Spirits Association, set up the Wine and Spirits Education Trust. The Company currently also sponsors the Wine Studies Centre at Plumpton College, thereby demonstrating a comprehensive interest in, and support of, wine education countrywide. This is evidenced in no small way, through the Company's Vintners's Scholarship awarded to the top WSET Diploma graduate, and three Travel Bursaries for those who excel at Advanced Certificate level.

In addition, the Company undertakes a wide range of charitable and educational works within the Greater London area.

Vintners's Hall, rebuilt after the Great Fire of 1666, is situated at the north side of Southwark Bridge and is, understandably, known as the "Spiritual Home of the Wine Trade". The Company also enjoys ownership of the swans on the Thames and takes part in "Swan Upping" every July.

The Vintners's Company is very proud of its association with wine education in general and the Wine and Spirits Education Trust in particular.

We are delighted to be able to assist in the sponsorship of this book, and we hope that you will find time to learn more about the Vintners's Company through our website: www.vintnershall.co.uk

The Master Vintner

Introduction

Welcome to *Wines and Spirits: Looking Behind the Label*.

It is impossible to tell what a wine will taste like simply from the label – however, it is possible to know what the wine should taste like, and this is what this book seeks to address. *Looking Behind the Label* takes as a starting point the most prominent informative words appearing on the label of a bottle of wine. This could be a grape variety, or it could be a region – these are very powerful indicators of style.

To keep things as simple as possible, we have focused on the grape varieties and regions that are most frequently encountered – so please excuse us if the more obscure wines are not mentioned. Similarly, you will not find specific information about producers, brands and vintages – such information is easily available in internet sites, magazines and newspapers. What remains is, I hope, 'timeless' content that will continue to be relevant even though the market and production of wine will change. I passed my WSET qualifications 25 years ago, and still keep my textbooks for reference!

Since the Wine & Spirit Education Trust was founded (in 1969), the interest in knowing more about wines and spirits has grown immensely. This is the case for people involved in making, distributing, retailing and serving wine, but also among enthusiastic consumers who are discovering more and more the fascinations of the world of wines and spirits.

So, for those readers who are on a WSET course, I wish you every success in the examination. For those who are not, why not visit our website at www.wsetglobal.com for details of courses that are available throughout the world.

I do hope that you enjoy reading this book. If you wish to go more deeply into the subject, with more in-depth coverage of wines by region, I would recommend that you progress to the WSET Advanced Certificate Course and its accompanying textbook: *Exploring the World of Wines and Spirits*.

Ian Harris
Chief Executive, Wine & Spirit Education Trust

1 Tasting and Evaluating Wine

Tasting wine rather than simply drinking it increases our appreciation of the wine by allowing us to examine it in detail. Although the process can seem repetitive at first, with practice it becomes a subconscious habit. Forcing us to put our sensations into words means the impression of the wine lingers longer in our memory. It also helps us communicate to other people what the wine is like, sometimes long after we have tasted it. This is an essential skill for anyone involved in the production, distribution or sale of wine. As we will see in Chapter 2, successful food and wine matching requires us to consider the separate components of the wine. The systematic approach to tasting, outlined below, shows us how to do this.

PREPARATION FOR TASTING

It is important that our impression of the wine is not altered by any outside influences. The ideal tasting room will be odour-free (no smells of cleaning products, tobacco, food or perfume), with good natural light, and white surfaces against which we can judge the appearance of our wines. Our tasting palate should be clean, and unaffected by tobacco, food, coffee, gum or toothpaste. Chewing a piece of bread can help remove any lingering flavours. Hayfever, colds and fatigue affect our ability to judge wines, because they affect our senses of taste and smell.

Many glasses have been developed to show different wines at their best. However, we need one type of glass in order to make fair comparisons between wines. At the WSET, we use the ISO glass, as illustrated. It has a rounded bowl that is large enough to swirl the wine. The sides slope inwards in a tulip shape to concentrate the aromas, and the stem allows us to hold the glass without warming the wine.

THE WSET SYSTEMATIC APPROACH TO TASTING (INTERMEDIATE)

This approach systematically describes aspects of a wine in the order we encounter them. Appearance first, then the nose, then the palate, and finally we may use our impressions to draw a conclusion about the quality of the wine.

Appearance

The main reason for looking at the appearance of a wine is that it can warn us of faults. If a wine is too old, has been badly stored, or the cork seal has failed, allowing air to damage the wine, then it is described as **out-of-condition**. This is the most common fault that shows itself in the appearance: out-of-condition wines will be dull in appearance, and will have at least a hint of brown, though a brown colour does not always indicate a faulty wine. (Brown hints can appear in healthy old wines, particularly those that have been aged for very long periods in oak.) Haziness may indicate a fault, or it could be that the wine has deliberately not been filtered before bottling (see Chapter 4).

It is worth making a quick note of the colour. Look at the intensity: is it particularly intense or pale? If it is a red wine, is it ruby (purply-red) or garnet (orangey-red)? Purple is an indication of youth; orange, amber and brown colours are indicators of age. However, bear in mind that some wines change colour more rapidly than

ISO tasting glass.

Tasting sample 50ml.

150 – 160mm

others, so no definitive conclusions about actual age can be reached. If it is a white wine, is it lemon (yellow with a hint of green) or gold (yellow with a hint of orange)? Green indicates youth; orange and brown indicate age. For rosé wines, a bright purply-pink indicates youth; orange and brown hints indicate age.

The colour of a wine from any particular region or grape variety depends greatly on the age of the wine, and the winemaking techniques used. As it is impossible to generalise about the appearance of these wines, the descriptions throughout the book limit themselves to describing wines as red, rosé or white, with very few exceptions. The following are examples of more precise descriptions of appearance:

- clear, intense ruby
- clear, medium-intensity, garnet
- clear, pale gold
- dull and cloudy, dark brown

(The last wine would almost certainly be faulty.)

Nose

The next step is to smell the wine. Swirl it in the glass to release as many aroma molecules as possible, then take a sniff. Make a note of the condition of the nose. Are there any off-notes? The most common fault that can be discovered on the nose is **cork taint**. At low levels, this can strip the wine of its fresh, fruity aromas. At its worst, it can add a pungent, unpleasant damp cardboard or musty smell to the wine. **Out-of-condition** wines will smell dull and stale, and may have excessive oxidative aromas (toffee, caramel or sherry). However, the presence of oxidative aromas does not always indicate a fault: some wines, such as Oloroso Sherry (see Chapter 24), are deliberately oxidised during production.

Assuming the wine is healthy, how intense are the aromas? Are they particularly pronounced, or are they light and hard to detect? Describing the smell is a more subjective aspect. It will depend greatly on your previous experiences. Some of the descriptions may sound fanciful at first. However, there are well-understood reasons why aromas such as butter, vanilla, rose or raspberry appear in some wines. Other aromas are less well understood, but wine tasters can be quite consistent in their use. What are the alternatives? Some writers avoid using aroma descriptors, but in order to evoke the wine their tasting notes often use words such as 'feminine', 'elegant', 'clumsy'. These words can be very appropriate, but difficult to define. A more scientifically

objective approach would involve naming the particular chemical compounds which are present, which is almost impossible to do accurately and would be useless to most wine drinkers!

On page 4 we have included a table of suggested aroma/flavour words, and how they might be grouped together. This is not an exhaustive list, but it is a very thorough starting point. We recommend that you taste the fruits, vegetables and spices, and smell the flowers, the leather, the bread and so on. Make your aroma-description vocabulary as wide and precise as possible. Always be aware, however, that one purpose of a tasting note is to help describe a wine to someone who has not tasted it. Terms such as 'the back of my garage' or 'the glue we used to use at school', while useful for a private tasting notebook, are unlikely to help describe the wine to many other people.

Palate

It is often said that tasting is an entirely subjective matter. It is true that our sensitivities to sweetness, acidity, tannins and certain aroma compounds differ. Our private experience of tasting the wines may be entirely different (how could we ever know?). However, even if we have different sensitivities to the components in a wine, we can usually agree which of any pair of wines is sweeter, more acidic, or more tannic. From this, it is a short step (though it requires a lot of tasting experience), before we can say whether a wine has medium, or particularly high or low levels of these components.

Different parts of the mouth have different

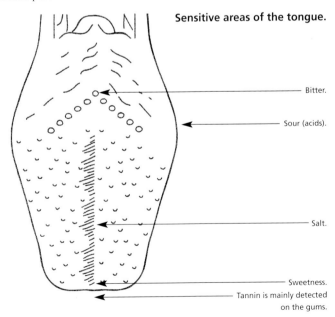

Sensitive areas of the tongue.

Bitter.

Sour (acids).

Salt.

Sweetness.
Tannin is mainly detected on the gums.

WSET® SYSTEMATIC APPROACH TO TASTING (INTERMEDIATE)

Appearance	Clarity	clear – dull
	Intensity	pale – medium – deep
	Colour	*White*: lemon – gold – amber *Rosé*: purple – orange *Red*: purple – ruby – garnet – tawny
Nose	Condition	clean – unclean
	Intensity	light – medium – pronounced
	Aroma	*characteristics*: fruit – floral – spice – vegetal – oak – other
Palate	Sweetness	dry – off-dry – medium – sweet
	Acidity	low – medium – high
	Tannin	low – medium – high
	Body	light – medium – high
	Flavour	*characteristics*: fruit – floral – spice – vegetal – oak – other
	Length	short – medium – long
Conclusion	Quality	poor – acceptable – good – very good – outstanding

AROMA AND FLAVOUR CHARACTERISTICS

Fruit	Citrus	grapefruit, lemon, lime
	Green Fruit	apple (green/ripe?), gooseberry, pear
	Stone Fruit	apricot, peach
	Red Fruit	raspberry, red cherry, plum, redcurrant, strawberry
	Black Fruit	blackberry, black cherry, blackcurrant
	Tropical Fruit	banana, kiwi, lychee, mango, melon, passion fruit, pineapple
	Dried Fruit	fig, prune, raisin, sultana
Floral	Blossom	elderflower, orange
	Flowers	perfume, rose, violet
Spice	Sweet	cinnamon, cloves, ginger, nutmeg, vanilla
	Pungent	black/white pepper, liquorice, juniper
Vegetal	Fresh	asparagus, green bell pepper, mushroom, black olive
	Cooked	cabbage, tinned vegetables (asparagus, artichoke, peas, etc.)
	Herbaceous	eucalyptus, grass, hay, mint, blackcurrant leaf, wet leaves
	Kernel	almond, coconut, hazelnut, walnut, chocolate, coffee
	Oak	cedar, medicinal, resinous, smoke, vanilla, tobacco
Other	Animal	leather, wet wool, meaty
	Autolytic	yeast, biscuit, bread, toast
	Dairy	butter, cheese, cream, yoghurt
	Mineral	earth, petrol, rubber, tar, stony/steely
	Ripeness	caramel, candy, honey, jam, marmalade, treacle, cooked, baked, stewed

Updates are made to the WSET Systematic Approach to Tasting each year. If you are using this book to prepare for a WSET examination, please consult your course specification or the WSET website, www.wsetglobal.com, for the most recent version.

levels of sensitivity to sweetness, acidity and tannins. Because of this, if we wish to extract the maximum information, it is important to swirl the wine around the mouth so that every part is exposed to it.

Sweetness is an indicator of how much sugar a wine contains, though wines made from very ripe grapes can have a slightly sweet flavour even when there is no sugar. Almost all red wines, and most white wines, are dry, that is, they contain almost no sugar. White wines that taste slightly sweet are described as 'off-dry'. The part of the tongue that is most sensitive to sweetness is the tip.

Acidity is what makes lemons taste sour. It causes the mouth to water, and its presence makes wines taste vibrant and refreshing. It is present in all wines, though levels in white wines are generally higher than acidity levels in reds. Certain varieties, such as Riesling and Sauvignon Blanc, give wines that are particularly high in acidity. Cool climates generally result in higher levels of acidity than hot climates. Acidity is very important for sweet wines. If it is too low, the wines taste oversweet, and cloying. Acidity is most strongly detected by the sides of the tongue.

Tannin is what makes strong black tea taste bitter and astringent. Tannins are present in grape skins, and their presence in a wine depends on the amount of skin contact during winemaking (see Chapter 3). White and rosé wines receive very little, if any, skin contact, so they rarely have any detectable tannin. Thick-skinned varieties (Cabernet Sauvignon, Syrah) have much higher tannin levels than thin-skinned ones (Pinot Noir, Grenache). High levels of soft ripe tannins may indicate a hot-climate wine. Note that astringent tannins from unripe grapes can cause a strong, mouth-drying sensation, even when their levels are low. The bitter flavours are most strongly tasted at the back of the tongue; the astringent sensations are most strongly felt on the gums. Soft, ripe tannins contribute to the viscosity and body of the wine.

Body is also sometimes described as 'mouth-feel'. It is the sensation of richness, weight or viscosity, and is a combination of the effects of alcohol, tannins, sugars and flavour compounds extracted from the skins. It is possible for a wine such as Beaujolais to be high in alcohol (13% abv), but still be light in body because it has very little tannin, and is lightly flavoured.

In contrast to sweetness, acidity, tannins and body, which are detected in the mouth, **flavour characteristics** are detected when aroma components in the wine evaporate off the tongue and rise up to the back of the nose. This is why we cannot taste properly with a cold. To help these volatile flavour components reach the nose, many tasters slurp the wine by drawing air in through their lips while tasting it. The groups of flavour descriptors are the same as those for the nose.

Length, also called the finish, is how long the flavours linger in the mouth after the wine has been swallowed or spat out. A long, complex finish is an indicator of quality (see below).

Conclusions

Finally, having described our wine, we may form an assessment of its quality. A good starting point is to ask yourself whether you like the wine or not. If you like it, how much do you like it, and what do you like about it? If you did not enjoy it, try to articulate what you did not like about it.

Of course, an objective assessment of quality goes beyond personal likes and dislikes. You may dislike a particular wine because you do not like acidic or oaky wines, for example, but other wine consumers do like these styles. The key question is, is it a good example of its type? This question becomes easier to answer as you gain more experience. Assuming the wine is not faulty (badly made, out-of-condition, affected by cork taint), many criteria can differentiate between a poor wine, an acceptable wine and a great wine. These include:

Balance. Fruitiness and sweetness alone can make a wine taste sickly or cloying. Acidity and tannin alone or in excess can make a wine taste hard, unpleasant or austere. In a good quality wine, the sweetness and the fruitiness will be in balance with the tannin and acidity.

Length. A balanced, pleasant finish where the flavours linger for several seconds is an indicator of a high quality wine. For inferior wines, the flavours may disappear almost instantly leaving no lingering impression, or the flavours that linger may be unpleasant.

Intensity. Dilute flavours can indicate a poor wine. However, extreme, intense flavours are not necessarily a sign of quality, because they can easily upset the balance of a wine and make it difficult to drink.

Complexity. Lesser wines often have one or two simple flavours and quickly become boring. The greatest wines generally have many different flavours.

Expressiveness. Lesser wines taste as if they could come from anywhere and be made with any grape variety. Great wines express characteristics of their grape variety and/or their region of production (climate, soils, traditional winemaking techniques). In a few rare cases, the individual vineyard can be identified from the flavours of the wine.

Selecting and recommending wines

When choosing wines for an occasion, or making a recommendation, it is important to take account of the **tastes** and and **preferences** of those who will be consuming the wine (and the price requirements of whoever is paying!). When catering for large numbers of people with diverse or unknown tastes, it is wise to avoid extreme styles of wines such as Alsace Gewurztraminer or Barolo, and it can be a good idea to offer alternatives (dry/medium, red/white/rosé). When matching a wine to an **occasion,** remember that except for exceptional circumstances, the wine should not be the centre of attention. However, it should be of an appropriate quality: for special occasions it can be a good idea to trade up to a premium quality wine. However, very fine, rare, special bottles may be best saved for a modest occasion where they can be given the attention they deserve: they will make that occasion a special one. Food is an important consideration when selecting a wine for an occasion. Matching wine with food is the subject of the next chapter.

Tips for how to serve wine and how much you may need to supply are in the appendices.

2 Matching Wine with Food

Most wines are produced as an accompaniment to food, and there are many established guidelines for matching wine with food successfully. Originally wine styles evolved to complement the cuisine of a region, so this is often a good starting point for finding a good wine and food combination. There is no single choice of wine that must be drunk with a certain dish, but some are definitely a better match than others.

THE BASIC CONSIDERATIONS

To achieve the best match it is necessary to analyse the basic components in both the wine and the food. The principle is to try to balance these, so that neither the food nor the wine overpowers the other. The main elements to consider are:

- Match the weight/richness of the food and the body of the wine.
- Match the flavour intensity of the food and the flavour intensity of the wine.
- Match acidic foods with high-acid wines.
- Match sweet foods with sweet wines.
- Avoid combining oily or very salty foods with high-tannin red wines.

These guidelines will help avoid wine and food clashes, or one overpowering the other. Other considerations can help us find wine and food combinations where the wine and the food really enhance each other.

- Pair 'chewy' meat with tannic wines.
- Pair salty foods with sweet or high-acid wines.
- Pair fatty and oily food with high-acid wines.
- Match or contrast flavour characteristics of the food and the wine.

Weight/Richness of the Food and the Wine

The first and most important element to consider should be to match the weight of the food with that of the wine. Rich heavyweight foods, like game, roast meats and red meat casseroles, need a full-bodied wine. Powerful red wines are often the favoured choice, although it is the body of the wine which is the most important consideration rather than its colour or flavour. For many meat dishes, a rich full-bodied white wine is a better match than a lighter red wine. Lighter food, such as plain white meat or fish, is complemented by more delicate wine. Although white wines are the normal choice, light-bodied, low-tannin red wines can also be successful.

Always remember the contribution of the sauce. A rich creamy sauce will need a wine of sufficient body to match the food and flavours that will complement the smooth creamy, buttery taste.

Flavour Intensity of the Food and the Wine

After weight, the next most important element to consider is flavour and how intense that flavour is. Flavour intensity, although similar to weight, is not the same. Think of a food that has a lot of weight but is low in flavour, say a plate of plain boiled potatoes or plain boiled rice; both are heavy in weight but light in flavour. At the other end of the scale think of a plate of raw, thinly sliced red or green peppers; these are high in flavour but light in weight. Wines can be the same. Riesling, for example, makes a lightweight wine that is intensely flavoured, while Chardonnay makes full-bodied, heavyweight wines that can be low in flavour. Delicate wines and strong-flavoured foods do not match.

It is worth considering the way the food has been cooked. If a food is cooked by a moist, gentle method such as steaming, it will require a lighter-flavoured wine than a food that is roasted, which will require a wine that is fuller-bodied and more robust in flavour because the method of cooking adds intensity of flavours to the food. A slow-cooked dish that has been braised or stewed will be weightier and need intensely flavoured wines, because the food's flavours are intensified by the method of cooking.

Acidity in the Food and the Wine

Sour flavours in food make wines taste less acidic, and therefore less vibrant and refreshing. For this reason, any acidity found in the food should be matched by acidity in the accompanying wines. Acidity is something we rarely think about in food. Tomatoes, lemons, pineapples, apples and vinegar are all high in acidity. One of the characteristics of Italian red wines is their noticeable acidity. This is because much Italian cuisine is dominated by two ingredients – tomatoes and olive oil, and other acidic ingredients such as lemons, vinegar (balsamic) and wine are often used – hence wines that go with Italian food need high acidity.

Vinaigrette is an example of acidity being added to a dish. The oil needs to be cut by the sharpness of acidity, so when making a vinaigrette you blend olive oil and vinegar together. Dishes dominated by tart acidic flavours, like lemon, lime or vinegar, can be difficult and require care when matching as they will overpower many wines.

Sweetness in the Food and the Wine

Dry wines can seem tart and over-acidic when consumed with any food with a degree of sweetness. Sweet food is best with wine which has a similar or greater degree of sweetness; the sweeter the food, the sweeter the wine needs to be. Late-harvest wines, especially botrytis-affected wines, and sweet Muscat-based wines (see Chapter 23) are the ideal choice for puddings.

Oil, Salt and Tannins

Tannin in combination with oily fish can result in an unpleasant metallic taste, so the general recommendation is to avoid red wines with fish. However, low tannin reds are fine with meaty fish. Wines with a high tannin content can also taste bitter with salty foods.

'Chewy' Meat and Tannins

Tannin in red wine reacts with protein. Foods with a high protein content, particularly rare red meat, will soften the effects of the tannin on the palate. This is why wines from high-tannin grape varieties, such as Cabernet Sauvignon or Syrah/Shiraz, go well with roast meats, stews and steaks.

Light, fruity red wines with low levels of tannin, like Beaujolais and Valpolicella, will complement white meats because these are low in proteins and lighter than meats such as lamb and beef.

Salty Foods and Sweet or High-Acid Wines

Salty foods are enhanced by a touch of sweetness. Think of classic combinations like prosciutto and figs. The same works with wine. Roquefort cheese and Sauternes, or Port and Stilton are famous matches. Salty foods also benefit from a little acidity. Salty foods such as olives, oysters and other shellfish go best with crisp, dry, light-bodied white wines. Although neither sweet nor high in acid, Fino Sherry (see Chapter 24) is a classic accompaniment for olives or salted nuts.

Fatty/Oily Foods and High-Acid Wines

Wines with a good level of acidity can be superb with rich, oily foods, such as pâté. For example, Sauternes works well with foie gras. Here the weight of both wine and food are similar, and the acidity in the wine helps it cut through the fattiness of the food. This is also an example of matching a sweet wine to a savoury food. Crisp wines such as Riesling and unoaked Barberas can make a good match with fatty meats such as duck and goose. Foods that have been cooked by frying will need wines with high acidity, because the method of cooking increases the fat content.

Key Flavours in the Food and the Wine

The flavour character of a food can sometimes complement or contrast with flavours in the wine. Often the dominant flavour of the food is in the sauce.

Smoked foods need wines with enough character to cope with the strength of the smoking. Lightly smoked salmon is a classic partner for Brut Champagne; smoked meats like pork can benefit from some slight sweetness in the wine like that found in some German Rieslings; smoky barbecued flavours suit powerful oaked wines like Australian Shiraz. The stronger the smoke, the greater the oak can be.

Spicy foods are best matched by wines that are made from really ripe, juicy fruit, either unoaked or very lightly oaked (many spices accentuate the flavours of oak). Wines such as New Zealand Sauvignon Blanc can work well with highly spiced foods, as can ripe Chilean Merlot. Spicy wines, such as Gewurztraminer can also complement spicy dishes. (When describing a wine, the term 'spice' can mean a number of different aromas and flavours such as white pepper, black pepper, cloves, cinnamon, nutmeg and ginger.) Hot spices like chilli reduce the sweetness in wine and can make dry red wines seem more astringent.

Fruity flavours in food can be matched with fruity/floral wines. For example, a Muscat might be paired with a fruit salad.

These guidelines and recommendations should avoid disastrous combinations, but individual taste is the final consideration. Experimentation can yield surprising results.

Factors Affecting Wine Style, Quality and Price

3

Wine is made from the fruit of the grape vine. The main factors that determine how a wine will taste are: the grape variety used; the environment in which it is grown (climate and weather, soil and slope); the care with which the grapes are grown and harvested; how the wine is made; and how it is matured (including bottle-age). Many of the factors that affect quality have a cost effect and will influence the final selling price of a bottle of wine.

GRAPE VARIETY

Just as there are different kinds of apples and potatoes, there are different varieties of grapes. Over centuries, particular vines have been chosen that have desirable characteristics (pleasant flavour, high yields, and resistance to disease and so on). These chosen vines include those that are most well known to us, such as Chardonnay and Cabernet Sauvignon, as well as many hundreds of others. The type of grape used determines a large part of the character of the wine: as well as affecting the flavours and colour of the wine, different grape varieties have different levels of sugar (for alcohol), acidity and tannins. The particular characteristics of different major grape varieties are discussed in the sections covering those varieties. Not all Chardonnays, or Cabernet Sauvignons, taste the same or cost the same. This is because the other factors have an important effect on style and quality.

ENVIRONMENT

In order to grow and produce a crop of ripe, healthy grapes, a vine needs **carbon dioxide** (CO_2), **sunlight, water, warmth** and **nutrients**. The first of these is found in the air (much of it is breathed out by animals), but the availability of the other four is affected by the vine's environment. In particular, climate and weather affect sunlight, heat and water, and the soil affects warmth and water, as well as the availability of nutrients.

Climate describes what weather conditions (temperatures, rainfall, sunshine) we may expect in a typical year.

Warmth and sunlight can have a dramatic effect on the flavour of ripe grapes. Some grape varieties (such as Cabernet Sauvignon) need a lot of heat to ripen fully. If the grapes have not fully ripened, wines from these varieties will taste

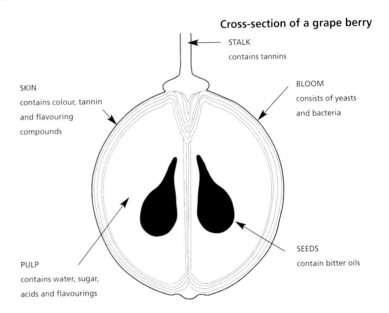

Cross-section of a grape berry

STALK
contains tannins

SKIN
contains colour, tannin and flavouring compounds

BLOOM
consists of yeasts and bacteria

PULP
contains water, sugar, acids and flavourings

SEEDS
contain bitter oils

excessively sour, astringent, bitter and lacking in fruit flavours. Other grapes (such as Sauvignon Blanc and Pinot Noir) need a moderate or cool climate otherwise they over-ripen and lose their refreshing fruit character and acidity. Unpleasant jammy or raisiny cooked flavours may then dominate the wine, or it may simply taste bland. A few grapes (such as Chardonnay) can make interesting wines in hot, moderate and cool climates. The flavours in the wine give clues as to the climate; and there are more details on how climate affects the flavour and style of wines in the separate grape variety chapters. In general, we may say that:

- hot climate: more alcohol, fuller body, more tannin, less acidity.
- cool climate: less alcohol, lighter body, less tannin, more acidity.

The grape contains all the materials needed to make wine: sugar (for alcohol), water, acids, flavours, colour and tannins. The quantity and quality of these components depend on the grape variety, the environment where it has ripened, and how it has been grown.

MAIN EFFECTS ON CLIMATE		
Latitude	Closer to the equator e.g. Australia, South Africa	Hotter
	Further from the equator e.g. Germany, New Zealand South Island	Cooler
Altitude	Higher e.g. the best areas of Argentina	Cooler
The sea	Warm ocean currents e.g. Western Europe	Hotter
	Cold ocean currents e.g. California, Chile, the South African Cape, southern Australia	Cooler
Regions in the centre of large landmasses (e.g. Burgundy, central Spain) have hotter summers and colder winters than regions near the coast (e.g. Bordeaux)		

As weather conditions vary from one year to the next, the **weather** of each particular year affects the style and quality of wines from that year. The most important time is the growing season, particularly when the grapes are ripening. Extreme weather conditions such as hail, high winds, floods and late frosts can cause problems with the size and quality of the crop. Hail in particular can cause a great deal of damage to ripening grapes and to vines. Once the skins of grapes have been damaged, they are very susceptible to rot. Unusually cool or hot weather can affect the style and quality of the wines produced in a given year (vintage). Vintages are most important in regions such as Bordeaux and Champagne, where the weather varies greatly from one year to the next. Modern grape growing and winemaking techniques mean that even in these regions, differences between vintages are becoming less pronounced, and there are fewer bad years. Blending of varieties, or between different sites, villages or even regions, is a useful way to keep style and quality consistent from one year to the next. This is especially important for branded wines.

Sunlight

Sunlight is the source of the energy that allows the grape to combine carbon dioxide and water into sugar. From a winemaking perspective, these sugars are the most important part of a grape for it is these that are fermented to become alcohol. Quite simply, without sunlight, carbon dioxide and water, there would be no grape sugars; and without grape sugars there would be no wine. In regions far away from the equator, vines can receive more sunlight by being planted on slopes that angle them towards the sun, or above rivers that reflect sunlight. In sunny regions, this is unnecessary.

Water

Water can come from rain, or from the ground, or from irrigation. Too much water can cause grapes to become bloated. This may result in bigger crops, but the flavours and sugars will be diluted, and the wine will have less alcohol, body and flavour. In areas where rainfall is high, such as much of Europe, the best vineyards are on slopes or soils, such as gravel or chalk, which drain water away quickly. In regions where there is insufficient rainfall, such as many parts of the New World, irrigation is essential if the vine is to survive. For the highest quality wines, just enough water is provided to sustain sugar production. For cheaper wines, irrigation will be used to increase the size of the crop. Although a supply of water is essential for wine production, too much rain can cause problems. Wet conditions can encourage rot. Rain and hail can damage vines and grapes.

Warmth

Warmth is needed for the production of sugars – but not too little or too much. If the weather is too cool or too hot, sugar production slows and can stop. This is one of the reasons why most of the world's vineyards are found in a temperate zone between 30 and 50° from the equator. A vine can keep itself cool by evaporating water through its leaves. This process occurs more rapidly in hot, dry, conditions. In extreme cases, the vine may shut down its leaves to prevent the plant drying out, so, although there is warmth and heat, no sugars are produced. The main factors affecting warmth are climate and weather. In addition, soils vary in their ability to absorb or reflect warmth. Dry, stony soils are generally warmer than wet clay soils, for example.

Here, bunches are being removed from the vine before they have ripened. This will reduce yields, but ensures that the remaining bunches have a better chance of ripening fully and evenly. The quality of the grapes, and the resulting wine is improved, but such activities increase production costs.

Nutrients

The sugars produced by the leaves do not just provide sweetness in the grapes: they are the building blocks for the whole vine. In a sense, almost the entire plant is built out of the material provided by the carbon dioxide in the air, and the water obtained via its roots. However, the plant also needs tiny amounts of nutrients, in the right balance. These are provided by the soil. Grapevines are very tolerant, and will grow in a wide range of soils. In general, provided there are sufficient nutrients, poorer soils result in better quality grapes.

GRAPEGROWING

Over the course of the vineyard year, the two main factors that affect the quality and style of the raw grape material are the degree of care that is taken in the vineyard, and control of yields.

There are many **vineyard activities** that can help all the grapes ripen fully, at the same time. These include careful pruning, controlling the number of bunches of grapes on each vine, and careful positioning of the leaves to increase or lower the temperature of the grape bunches, or their degree of exposure to sunlight. These techniques all use expensive labour, which increases the cost as well as the quality. The other extreme is minimal pruning and maximum mechanisation, which is only appropriate in regions with suitably large, flat vineyards.

Yields also have an effect on quality. Lower yields generally result in riper grapes with more concentrated flavours, but controlling yields by limiting the number of grape bunches takes time. Also, because the crop is smaller, each kilogram costs more to grow and will have to sell for a higher price if the effort is to be worthwhile. The other extreme is to maximise yields using irrigation to fill the grapes with water, with the result that flavours and sugars are diluted. The resulting wine will be cheap, but probably not very interesting. Most wines lie somewhere between these two extremes.

In addition to the effects of soil and aspect, climate and weather, and care in the vineyard, some **pests and diseases** are bad for the production of healthy grapes:

- Animal pests (including birds and insects) can damage shoots, buds, leaves, and may eat the grapes.
- Attacks of fungal diseases such as mildew or rot can damage green parts of the vine as well as leading to spoiled grapes.

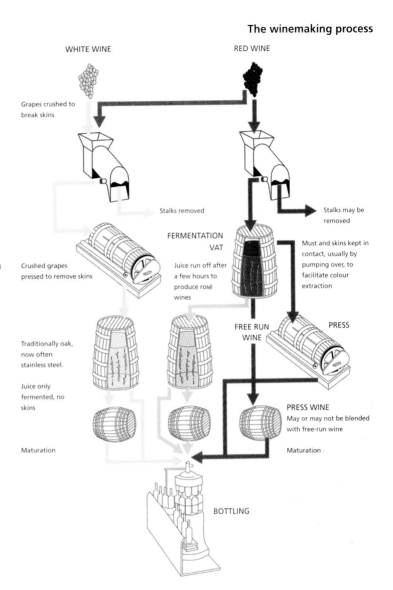

The winemaking process

WHITE WINE

RED WINE

Grapes crushed to break skins

Stalks removed

Stalks may be removed

FERMENTATION VAT

Crushed grapes pressed to remove skins

Juice run off after a few hours to produce rosé wines

Must and skins kept in contact, usually by pumping over, to facilitate colour extraction

FREE RUN WINE

PRESS

Traditionally oak, now often stainless steel.

Juice only fermented, no skins

PRESS WINE
May or may not be blended with free-run wine

Maturation

Maturation

BOTTLING

- Long-term diseases caused by fungi, bacteria or viruses can affect the health of the vine, reducing yields and inhibiting ripening. Some eventually lead to the death of the vine.

The **harvest** occurs once the grapes have ripened. In larger vineyards on flatter sites, harvesting will generally be done by machines which shake the grapes off their stems. Where whole bunches of grapes are needed, the grapes must be hand-harvested. Steep sites with difficult access must also be hand-harvested, and regions where labour is cheap may hand-harvest, even where machines could be used. Top quality wines can be made from both machine-harvested and hand-harvested grapes.

Machine-harvested grapes are undergoing a hand-selection process to remove any rotten or unripe grapes. This is labour-intensive, and increases production costs, but the effect on quality can be dramatic.

WINEMAKING

The most important part of this process is fermentation. When yeasts feed on sugars in the grape juice, they produce alcohol, carbon dioxide and heat and change the flavours of the grape juice into those of wine.

The flesh of almost all wine grape varieties is white. The colour of red and rosé wines is obtained by soaking the coloured skins in the fermenting juice. If the skins are removed at an early stage, there is little or no colour. This is how rosé wines are made from black grapes. White wine can be made from black or white grapes. Red wine can only be made from black grapes.

White Wines

For white wines, the grapes are usually **crushed** to break the skins before they are **pressed** to separate the juice from the skins. Yeast is added. This will usually be a commercially obtained yeast culture, which gives predictable results. Some winemakers choose not to use commercial yeasts: they believe that the 'natural' yeasts that dwell in the vineyard and winery give more interesting results.

The must is transferred to a **fermentation** vessel (usually a stainless steel tank, but some winemakers use oak barrels or open-topped concrete or wooden fermenters). White wines are then fermented at low temperatures (typically 15–20° C), to preserve delicate fruit aromas. This takes between two and four weeks.

Sweetness in white wines is caused by unfermented sugar. Sweet wines are discussed in Chapter 23.

Red Wines

Black grapes for red wines are **crushed** to release the juice, then the juice and skins are put in the fermenting vessel together. **Fermentation** takes place at a higher temperature for red than for white wine (25–30° C). Alcohol helps the **extraction** of colour, tannins and flavours from the skins. In order to keep the juice in contact with the skin, the juice may be pumped over the floating skins or the skins may be 'punched down' into the juice. The amount of colour and tannin in the finished wine depends on how long the wine is kept in contact with the skins. This may be for more than two weeks for richly-flavoured wines such as top quality Bordeaux, as little as five days for light wines such as Beaujolais. It also depends on how much tannin, colour and flavour is in the skins – some black grape varieties are naturally light in colour and tannins. Hot climates encourage higher colour and tannin levels in the grapes.

When enough colour and tannin have been extracted, the free-run wine is drawn off. The skins are then **pressed**, yielding a further quantity of wine, known as the 'press wine'. Press wines contain higher levels of tannin, and may be blended with free-run wine to produce the style required.

Rosé Wines

Like red wines, rosé wines must be made from black grapes. The method of production is similar to that for red wines, but they are fermented at a lower temperature (15–20° C). They must also have a much shorter period of grapeskin contact (12 to 36 hours). Pink wines labelled as 'blush' Zinfandel or 'blush' Grenache are made this way.

Oak Flavours

Many wines receive some oak contact, often in the form of staves (small planks) or chips (large splinters) added to a vat. Extra money pays for better quality staves or chips. The very cheapest method of adding oak flavours is to use oak essence. In the finest wines all oak contact must be achieved by fermenting or ageing the wine in oak barrels. If a wine is fermented or aged in oak, a large premium has to be paid, particularly if the oak is new, because oak is expensive. French oak is more expensive than American oak, but tends to give more subtle, toast and nutty flavours, whereas the American oak gives sweet coconut and vanilla. A further premium is also to be paid where the highest-quality air-dried staves and expert cooperage is sought. Looking after a wine in oak barrels, and ensuring it is always topped up to avoid air in the cask spoiling the wine, is labour-intensive and therefore expensive.

Fermentation, as well as ageing, in oak barrels is common for premium Chardonnay wines, including many of those made in Burgundy. It is impractical to ferment red wines in barrels, but many premium red wines are aged in oak.

MATURATION
Maturation can take place in barrels or large neutral wooden or stainless steel vats. It also takes place in the bottle after bottling. The most important changes that occur are the slow chemical reactions that can allow complex flavours to develop.

Maturation with Oxygen
We have already seen that new oak directly adds oaky flavours to the wine. Old oak vats do not directly add any flavours. However, in both cases, the vessel is porous and allows small amounts of oxygen to dissolve in the wine. This softens the tannins in red wines, making the wine taste smoother, and can cause flavours such as toffee, fig, hazelnut and coffee to develop.

Maturation without Oxygen
Bottles, cement and stainless steel vats are airtight and do not add any flavours, and the chemical reactions that occur are different to those in oak. In large stainless steel vats, the wine flavours stay almost unchanged for months. Changes occur faster in bottles because they are smaller. In bottles, in the absence of oxygen, the fresh fruit aromas of young wines change into cooked fruit, vegetal and animal notes (wet leaves, mushroom, leather).

Few wines improve in the bottle. It is common for the attractive fruit flavours simply to fade away, and nothing else to appear in their place. Often the animal and vegetal notes that develop will be unpleasant. For a few special wines, the fruit character remains while the other complex flavours develop around it. These wines are not easy to make, and are usually expensive to buy, but the flavours they offer are among the most rewarding of all wines. This brings us on to the question of price.

Granular untoasted oak (bottom left, looking like sawdust), oak beans (cubes, top right) and oak chips (with two different levels of toast) are used for adding oak characteristics to inexpensive wine, where the cost of new oak barrels would be prohibitive.

FACTORS AFFECTING COST
It is useful to summarise here some of the factors that affect the cost of producing a bottle of wine.

In the Vineyard
- Cost of vineyard land: sites with the greatest potential for quality can be vastly more expensive than ordinary locations.
- The degree to which the vineyard work is mechanised (almost impossible for very steep sites).
- The cost and availability of labour and/or equipment.
- Yield size and the degree of selection of grape material: discarding underripe or rotten grapes can be enormously labour intensive and, like yield control, must be justified in the final selling price.

In the Winery
- Winery equipment, and how efficiently this is used.
- Cost of barrels or other forms of oak flavouring.
- Ageing, which requires expensive storage facilities and ties up capital.

Red grape must is fermenting in large stainless steel vats. The juice must be kept in contact with the grapeskins to extract flavour, colour and tannins. Here this is achieved by pumping juice from the bottom of the vat over the floating mass of skins.

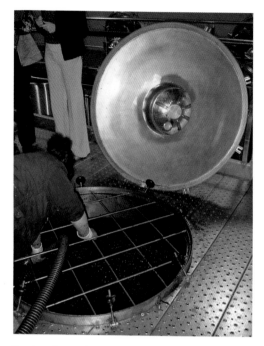

Packaging, Distribution and Sale
- Exchange rates can affect the final selling price for exported bottles.
- Packaging (bottles, etc.) and cartons for distribution. Unusual bottles cost extra.

- Transport costs (these are a surprisingly small part of the selling price of most wines: shipping long distances by sea is relatively inexpensive).
- The efficiency of the distributor and retailer, and the profit margins they expect. Low-volume, high-service distribution costs more.

Taxes and levies are also absorbed in the final retail price of a bottle of wine.

The ultimate factor that determines the selling price of a bottle of wine is how much the consumer is willing to pay. A bottle may be very expensive to produce, but if the quality does not match the price it will not sell. Marketing and the reputations of the producers, regions or brands can help sustain high prices, but if the quality fails to match consumers' expectations, then they move on to other wines. The reason that some regions continue to sell their wines at extremely high prices is that there are people who are prepared to pay high prices for those levels of quality. If the market disappeared, then the prices of these wines would fall or they would no longer be made.

Throughout this book, a distinction is made between wines that are produced in large volumes and/or sold at inexpensive prices, and premium quality wines, which are usually more expensive. Quality is discussed at the end of Chapter 1.

Understanding the Label

The most prominent pieces of information on most wine labels are usually the brand or producer, the country or region, and/or the variety of grape used to make the wine. Where a variety is not named, very often it can be deduced from the region (many European regions specify which grape varieties may be used, so that a wine from the Chablis appellation has to be made with Chardonnay, for example). Specific varieties and regions are covered in later chapters. This chapter will help you decode the rest of the information on the wine label.

4

PRODUCERS AND BRANDS

The name of the producer and/or the distributor will be found somewhere on the label. For some famous brands this will be the most prominent term. For other wines it will be hidden in the small print. Some brand names are created by or reflect the producer. These would include château or estate names, and large-scale brands such as Jacob's Creek and E & J Gallo Turning Leaf. Others are created by distributors or retailers. These include buyer's-own-brands (BOBs), such as wines sold under the name of a supermarket.

Port, Sherry, sparkling wine and most spirit categories, are dominated by a small number of large brands. For many consumers, the names of many grape varieties (Chardonnay, Shiraz…) and regions (Chablis, Sancerre…) act just like brands: they help the consumer make a decision by creating expectations of what the wine will be like. If those expectations are positive ones, and if the wines continue to meet the consumers' expectations, then those words on the label will help sell the wine.

VINTAGE

A vintage is usually stated. This is the year in which the grapes were harvested (see page 11). Most wines are best consumed while they are young and fresh, and should not be aged. For these wines, the vintage acts as an indication of how old the wine is. For a few prestigious, ageworthy wines, vintages makes a huge difference. For example, the price and quality of a 1990 wine from a good Bordeaux estate will be much higher than that of their 1991, because 1990 was an outstanding year with almost perfect weather, and 1991 a relatively poor one.

Seasons in the northern and southern hemispheres are inverted relative to each other. Wines from a given vintage will be made from grapes harvested in February, March or April (southern hemisphere) and August, September or October (northern hemisphere). As a result, southern hemisphere wines will be half a year older than northern hemisphere wines from the same vintage. This can make a difference for wines that are made to be consumed as young and fresh as possible, such as rosés and fruity unoaked whites.

QUALITY CLASSIFICATIONS AND REGIONAL LABELLING
European Union

The European Union (EU) divides its wines into two quality categories: QWPSRs (Quality Wines Produced in a Specified Region), and Table Wines. In theory, each QWPSR is unique, having a flavour that cannot be copied by any other wine. That uniqueness is caused by the place the grapes

PRODOTTO IN ITALIA ← Made in Italy.

Il Papavero ← Brand name.

VINO DA TAVOLA ROSSO ← Red Table Wine (*Vino da Tavola* is a basic quality wine i.e. not a QWPSR).

12,5%vol   IMBOTTIGLIATO DA MGM MONDO DEL VINO S.R.L. PRIOCCA - ITALIA   75cl ℮

	QWPSR (Quality Wine Produced in a Specified Region)	TABLE WINE WITH GEOGRAPHICAL DESCRIPTION	TABLE WINE
France	AOC (*Appellation d'Origine Contrôlée*)	*Vin de Pays*	*Vin de Table*
Germany	Prädikatswein QbA (*Qualitätswein bestimmter Anbaugebiete*)	*Deutscher Landwein*	*Deutscher Tafelwein*
Italy	DOCG (*Denominazione di Origine Controllata e Garantita*) DOC (*Denominazione di Origine Controllata*)	IGT (*Indicazione Geografica Tipica*)	*Vino da Tavola*
Spain	DOC (*Denominación de Origen Calificada*) DO (*Denominación de Origen*)	*Vino de la Tierra*	*Vino de Mesa*
Portugal	DOC (*Denominação de Origem Controlada*)	*Vinho Regional*	*Vinho de Mesa*

are grown, the grape varieties used, and the methods used to grow the grapes and make the wine. Therefore, for any named region of production, if the name appears on the label then the wine must be made within laws that specify the limits of the area, vinegrowing and winemaking techniques, and grape varieties. This is the system used in France, Italy, Spain and Portugal. Other EU wine-producing countries have, or are developing, systems along the same pattern. Germany's system is slightly different: as well as controlling the use of regional names, the wines can be graded according to the sugar levels in the

grapes. There is more detail on this in the sections covering German wines and sweet wines.

Because the laws for producing QWPSRs are restrictive, some producers prefer to make wines in the Table Wine category. This allows the use of non-traditional varieties (e.g. Chardonnay in the south of France). Ordinary Table Wine cannot name a variety or a vintage on the label. For export markets, Table Wines with Geographical Description are more common. They allow grape varieties and vintages to be named, and give an indication of the area of production. These are particularly important in Italy and southern France.

Other Countries

Although there is a category that corresponds roughly to 'Table Wine', these are rarely seen on international markets. Nearly all non-EU wines in the international market are 'Wine with Geographical Description'. Each country has developed its own way of dividing its vineyard areas into regions, zones, districts and so on, and controlling the use of regional names. These are described in Chapters 16 to 21.

A common misconception is that whereas EU wine production is closely regulated, in other countries producers are free to do what they like. It is true that outside of QWPSR wine production, producers have more freedom to experiment with vinegrowing and winemaking techniques such as irrigation and oak chips, and have more choice over which varieties to plant and where to grow them. Also, for most countries, where regions, vintages and varieties are named on the label, it is permissible to blend a small proportion of wine from other regions, vintages and varieties. However, all countries have their own legislation covering production techniques and use of label terms to prevent consumers from being misinformed or, worse, harming their health. In addition, any wine that is imported into the EU has to satisfy EU laws covering wine production techniques.

STYLE AND PRODUCTION TECHNIQUES

Apart from the variety, the region and the brand, the most common terms on wine labels are indications of style or production techniques. Those in English, such as 'hand-harvested', 'unoaked' or 'estate-bottled' are often self-explanatory. Some may need a little further clarification.

Vintage.

Brand name.

It is so common for Australian Chardonnays to have oak flavours, that those wines made without oak sometimes choose to say so on the label.

Region of origin (State within Australia).

2004
Edward's
Unwooded Lake
Chardonnay

Premium Chardonnay grapes were harvested in the cool of the night to capture elegant fruit character. Vibrant grapefruit and gooseberry flavours are balanced by ripe tropical fruit notes.
Serve chilled with Asian or chicken dishes.

NEW SOUTH WALES 24905

WINE OF AUSTRALIA
PRODUCED BY ROSSETTO WINES BEELBANGERA NSW 2680
AUSTRALIA SELECTED AND SHIPPED
BY THE EXCLUSIVE IMPORTER
DIRECT WINES LIMITED RG7 4PL UK
75cl e   13.5% vol

Oak-aged. The wine has been aged in oak vessels, of any size, which could be new or old.

Aged in new barriques. The wine has been aged in small (225 litre) oak barrels. New barrels will add lots of oak flavours to the wine, particularly when the barrels are small, because this maximises the surface area of the barrel in contact with the wine.

Barrel-fermented (white wines only). Fermenting the wine in oak results in a better integration of oak flavours in the wine, but it is more labour-intensive than simply ageing in oak, and therefore more expensive.

Oaked. This could indicate one of the above, but is more likely to indicate the use of oak staves or chips (see Chapter 3). (These last techniques are not permitted for QWPSRs and would not be used for any premium quality wines.)

Unfined/Unfiltered. Most wines are treated before bottling to remove anything that may cause haziness. Some argue that one side effect of fining and/or filtration is that too much of the character of the wine is stripped away, so a few producers prefer to minimise or avoid clarifying their wines before bottling. They may indicate this by stating on the label that the wines are unfined and/or unfiltered. These wines are more likely to form deposits in the bottle as they age, and are less likely to be perfectly clear and bright in the glass.

Grape variety.

Vintage.

Quality category: Table Wine with Geographical Description which permits the naming of a region (Oc), variety and vintage.

Brand name.

Vegetarian/Vegan. Fining agents used to clarify wines (see above) include isinglass (from sturgeons) and other animal proteins (such as egg white). Although none of the fining agent should remain in the wine after the process, it is not possible to guarantee this. For many vegetarians, the fact that an animal product has been used in the production process is a sufficient ethical basis to avoid the product. Wines labelled as suitable for vegetarians are not fined using isinglass. Vegan wines do not use any animal proteins for fining.

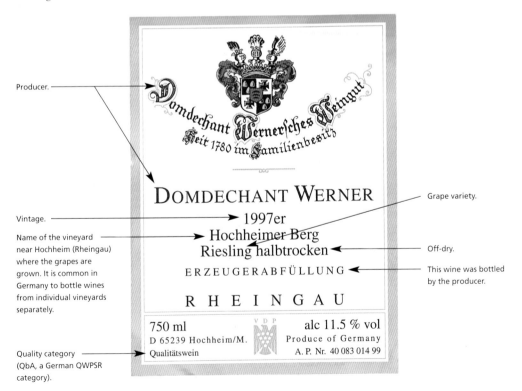

Producer.

Vintage.

Name of the vineyard near Hochheim (Rheingau) where the grapes are grown. It is common in Germany to bottle wines from individual vineyards separately.

Quality category (QbA, a German QWPSR category).

Grape variety.

Off-dry.

This wine was bottled by the producer.

ENGLISH	FRENCH	ITALIAN	SPANISH	PORTUGUESE	GERMAN
Wine	Vin	Vino	Vino	Vinho	Wein
Red	Rouge	Rosso	Tinto	Tinto	Rot
Rosé	Rosé	Rosato	Rosado	Rosado	Rosé
White	Blanc	Bianco	Blanco	Branco	Weiss
Dry	Sec	Secco	Seco	Seco	Trocken
Off-dry					Halbtrocken
Medium	Demi-sec	Semi-secco	Semi-seco	Semi-seco	Lieblich
Sweet	Moelleux Liquoreux Doux	Dolce	Dulce	Doce	Süss
Vintage/ harvest	Millésimé Vendange Récolte	Vendemmia Annata	Cosecha	Colheita	Ernte/Jahrgang

Organic. The wine has been made from grapes where synthetic fertilisers, pesticides and herbicides have not been used. Biodynamics is a system of organic grape growing and winemaking that links vineyard and winemaking activities to supposed 'natural cycles' of the Earth and wider universe.

For wine produced in countries where English is not the first language, many common label terms are simply translations of words such as 'red wine', 'medium-dry' and so on. Although phrases such as 'demi-sec' translate literally as 'medium-dry', the word refers to wines that we would describe as 'medium'.

Some countries have labelling terms that are peculiar to them, and more detail can be found in the chapters covering those countries. Note that outside of Italy, Spain and Portugal, words such as Reserve/Riserva/Reserva have no legal meaning, though companies often use them to indicate a better quality wine. Many other words, such as 'cuvée' and 'bin', although they do have a meaning (see the Glossary), are mostly meaningless when they are used on labels.

An **Estate** (**Château, Domaine, Weingut**) only uses grapes it has grown on its own land. A **Merchant**, or **Négociant**, blends together wines and grapes bought in from winemakers and grape farmers. The word 'Merchant', or 'Négociant' will not appear on the bottle, but most medium and large-volume brands follow this model. A **co-operative cellar** (cave coopérative, cantina sociale) is a winemaking facility whose ownership is shared by a number of grape farmers.

A more complete list of label terms is found in the Glossary.

Chardonnay

Chardonnay is not an aromatic grape variety. The delicacy of its fruit makes it suitable for expressing the oak and yeast-derived flavours described below, as well as subtle 'mineral' nuances that are associated with the properties of the soil in which the vines are grown.

5

THE FLAVOURS OF CHARDONNAY

Chardonnay is a white grape variety that is unusual because it can make attractive wines in regions ranging from cool (Chablis) to hot (Californian Central Valley). However, its fruit flavours vary greatly depending on where it is grown. In cool regions such as Chablis, it can offer green fruit (apple, pear) with citrus and occasionally vegetal notes (cucumber). In moderate regions, such as most of Burgundy and some premium New World regions, the wines may taste of white stone fruit (peach) with citrus notes and hints of melon. Warm regions, such as most New World sites, result in the expression of more tropical fruit notes (peach, banana and pineapple, and even mango and fig).

Many of the flavours commonly associated with Chardonnay wines come not from the grape variety, but from winemaking techniques. When they appear, the dairy (butter, cream) flavours are the side-products of a process called **malolactic** fermentation, which is sometimes used to soften harsh acids. The **lees** (dead yeast cells left behind after fermentation has finished) can also be stirred through the wine to add creamy texture and savoury flavours. Flavours of toast, vanilla and coconut occur because of **oak** treatment.

Not all premium Chardonnays taste of oak. Chardonnay has quite delicate flavours, and the regional characteristics the fruit can display are easily obliterated by excess oak. Wines such as Chablis work well because of their purity of fruit and little or no use of oak. Where the fruit is of sufficient quality, the wine can be fermented and aged in small new oak barrels and the oak and fruit will balance each other.

Chardonnay wines tend to be quite full-bodied, with a weighty, creamy texture. The best Chardonnays age well, developing honeyed nutty, savoury complexity.

PREMIUM CHARDONNAY REGIONS
White Burgundy

The classic region for Chardonnay wines, and arguably where this grape variety finds its highest

Premium Chardonnay vineyard in South Africa. Rose plants at the end of the rows give an early warning of mildew.

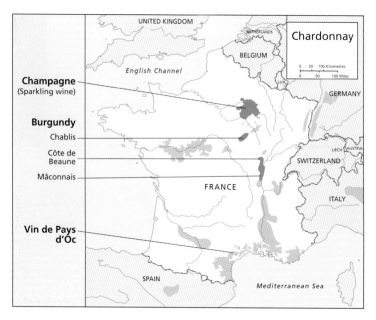

Chardonnay wines come mainly from the southern half (known as the Côte de Beaune), and are usually sold under the name of the village from which the grapes originate. The most famous of these are Meursault and Puligny-Montrachet. Complexity and body are often added to these wines by fermenting them in small oak barrels, and ageing them in contact with the yeast left over from fermentation. The resulting wines are full-bodied, and offer a complex succession of different flavours including citrus, white stone and tropical fruit, oak, spice and savoury notes. Chardonnay wines from the Le Montrachet vineyard are judged by many to be the very finest dry white wines in the world. They have prices to match.

The **Mâconnais** is the most southerly major district for White Burgundy. This is a source of large volumes of moderately priced, light, fruity (melon, citrus) Chardonnay wines, most of which see little or no oak and are sold as **Mâcon. Pouilly-Fuissé** offers full-bodied Chardonnay wines, often with tropical fruit (pineapple, melon) and oak flavours. These come from a series of steep suntrap slopes at the far south of the district.

Other Premium Chardonnay Regions

In **Australia**, the main regions for premium Chardonnay are the Hunter Valley Region (New South Wales), several cool parts of Victoria, the Limestone Coast Zone (including the Padthaway Region) and Adelaide Hills Region in South Australia, and the Margaret River Region in Western Australia. The Hunter Valley is a hot region, producing oaky wines with tropical fruit flavours (melon, fig). The cool Adelaide Hills Region produces Chardonnays with very high acid levels, and aromatic, vegetal and citrus

expression (certainly its most expensive) is Burgundy, in eastern France. The word 'Chardonnay' rarely appears on the labels of these wines, and they are labelled according to the region, the district, the village or sometimes the vineyard from which the grapes originate. The main districts for Chardonnay are Chablis, the Côte d'Or, and the Mâconnais.

Chablis is a cool district. The bone-dry wines it produces have high acidity and can be quite austere, with green fruit and citrus notes. Its special limestone soils give a recognisable smoky, flinty, mineral signature. These mineral characteristics are more pronounced in wines labelled *Premier Cru* or *Grand Cru*. With very few exceptions, oak flavours are not detectable in these wines.

The **Côte d'Or** is the heart of Burgundy.

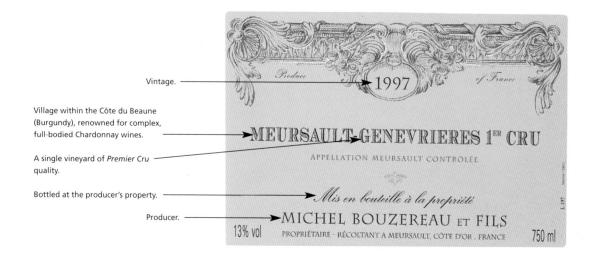

Vintage.

Village within the Côte du Beaune (Burgundy), renowned for complex, full-bodied Chardonnay wines.

A single vineyard of *Premier Cru* quality.

Bottled at the producer's property.

Producer.

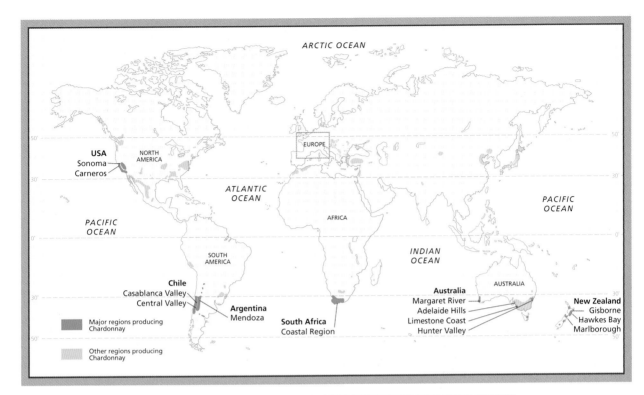

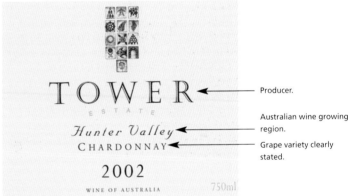

Producer.

Australian wine growing region.

Grape variety clearly stated.

(grapefruit) aromas. The classic Australian Chardonnay style has pronounced fruit and oak flavours, but unoaked and lightly oaked versions are becoming more common.

Production in **New Zealand** is too small to offer Chardonnay in the very lowest price brackets. Although it does have some large-volume brands, regions such as Hawkes Bay, Gisborne and Marlborough really come into their own as sources of premium Chardonnay fruit, with high natural acidity. Most of the best wines have pronounced oak flavours.

Chardonnay is grown widely throughout the premium wine-growing regions of **California**. Most premium Chardonnay comes from one of the regions lying between the Californian Coastal Range and the Pacific. Cool breezes and morning mists slow ripening, and the long ripening period allows intense, complex flavours to build up. The wines may be labelled simply as 'Coastal', or they may state a more specific location (such as Sonoma County or Carneros). Some premium producers even follow the Burgundian model by bottling their wines in small quantities according to the individual vineyard. California Chardonnays vary widely in style. Many are very full-bodied, with intense, rich citrus and ripe peach flavours, and heavily oaked. Others can be very savoury and reminiscent of Côte d'Or Burgundy.

In **Chile**, although some very high quality

Chardonnays are produced in the Central Valley, the Casablanca Valley north of Santiago is establishing itself as the premium Chardonnay subregion. Cool sea breezes and morning fogs slow ripening and allow time for flavours to build up, while acids are retained. Banana and melon flavours are often enhanced by barrel fermentation and ageing.

In **Argentina** there are some premium Chardonnay sites within the province of Mendoza, taking advantage of high altitude and cool night-time temperatures to help produce wines with intense fruit flavours.

South Africa, particularly in the cooler coastal parts such as the Walker Bay ward, is a source of some very fine Chardonnays.

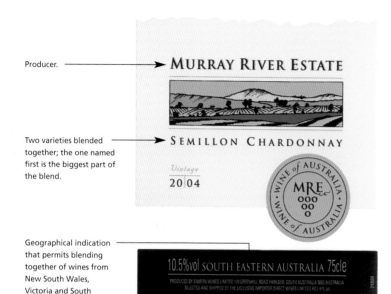

Producer.

Two varieties blended together; the one named first is the biggest part of the blend.

Geographical indication that permits blending together of wines from New South Wales, Victoria and South Australia, used for many inexpensive Australian wines.

BULK-PRODUCTION REGIONS FOR INEXPENSIVE CHARDONNAY

Chardonnay wines are very popular on international markets. Premium vineyard sites for Chardonnay are limited in area. Fortunately for Chardonnay-lovers, this is a grape variety that can tolerate a wide range of soils and climates, and can still show some of its soft texture and buttery-melon fruit flavours even at high yields. In order to hit low price points and still make a profit, producers need to make large volumes and take advantage of economies of scale in production, distribution and marketing. In order to obtain large volumes, wines from a number of sites may be blended together. The wine will be sold simply as coming from South Eastern Australia,

Western Cape, California, Central Valley (Chile) or Vin de Pays d'Oc. Chardonnay wines are also found at inexpensive prices in the Loire (Vin de Pays du Val de Loire), Southern Italy, Argentina and Hungary.

Generally, large-volume Chardonnays will be fermented, blended and stored in stainless steel vats until they are ready for packaging and sale. Oak flavours are often added in the form of staves or chips, though occasionally a proportion of the wine may be fermented or aged in oak barrels.

CHARDONNAY IN BLENDS

Chardonnay produces its finest still wines unblended. For the low-price, high-volume market, other grape varieties that are more widely available at a lower price may be used to stretch the Chardonnay component. The classic example of this is Semillon-Chardonnay (or Chardonnay-Semillon, depending on which variety dominates) from Australia. Semillon can provide some acidity and refreshing citrus notes to this blend, but its main purpose is to enable a wine with the word 'Chardonnay' on the label to hit a low price point. In South Africa and California, Colombard-Chardonnay and Chardonnay-Chenin Blanc blends work in much the same way.

Similarly, in European regions, unfashionable local grape varieties may be blended with Chardonnay to make a marketable wine, providing a viable outlet for grapes that may otherwise struggle to find a buyer.

One other grape variety that does seem to provide a successful pairing is Viognier. Its oily texture and full body merge well with Chardonnay, and the aromatic Viognier gives a little extra peachy, floral character to the wine.

Pinot Noir

Pinot Noir is very fussy about where it is grown, which makes it a very difficult variety for grape growers. However, it is a very easy variety to drink: unlike some other black grape varieties, such as Cabernet Sauvignon, many Pinot Noir wines have soft, light tannins and do not need time in the bottle to evolve attractive flavours. Instead, they are enjoyable to drink at all stages of their life.

6

THE FLAVOURS OF PINOT NOIR

Pinot Noir is a black grape variety with thin skins, and the resulting wines are usually light in colour with low to medium levels of tannin. In hot regions, it loses its delicate flavours, and the wines are excessively jammy. It likes moderate or cool climates, though in regions that are too cool, the grapes will not ripen and the wines will have excessive vegetal flavours (cabbage, wet leaves). In a few regions, the right balance is found, and the resulting wines display red fruit (strawberry, raspberry, cherry), with vegetal and animal nuances (wet leaves, mushroom, gamey-meaty aromas).

Some Pinot Noirs are able to develop great complexity with age. However, except for the very best wines from Burgundy, most Pinot Noirs are best consumed while they are youthful and fruity.

It is common to age the best Pinot Noirs in oak, but the toast and vanilla notes of new oak can easily overpower this variety's delicate flavours.

PREMIUM PINOT NOIR REGIONS
Red Burgundy

The classic region for Pinot Noir wines is in Burgundy (Bourgogne). This is where Pinot Noir's fussiness is most fully exploited: wines from the different villages show slightly different aspects of this variety, so they are given their own appellations. A **Bourgogne AC** should be a medium-bodied red with a balance of red-fruit and savoury aromas, light tannins and medium to high acidity. Wines from the individual villages, such as **Gevrey-Chambertin**, **Nuits-Saint-Georges**, **Beaune** and **Pommard**, generally offer more intensity, complexity and length, particularly those from *Premier Cru* vineyard sites within the villages. *Grand Cru* Red Burgundies, such as **Le Chambertin** are the most powerful, long-lived and complex Pinot Noir wines in the world. They sell at very high prices because of their quality and rarity.

Pinot Noir bunch at the moment of *véraison:* this is the point when the grapes stop expanding, and colours, sugars and flavours start to build up as the grapes ripen.

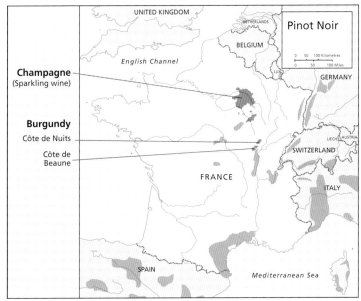

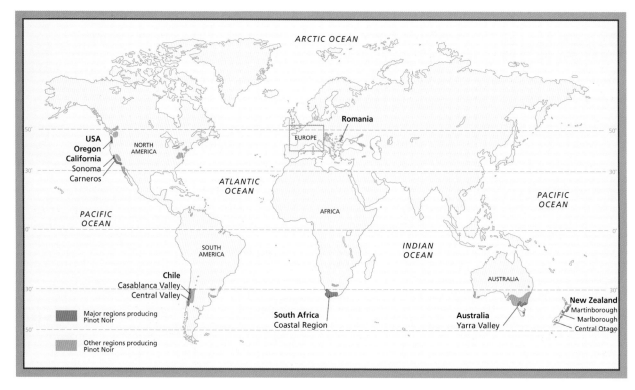

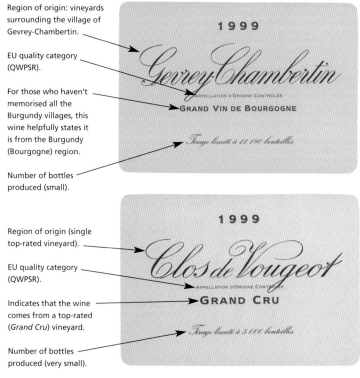

Region of origin: vineyards surrounding the village of Gevrey-Chambertin.

EU quality category (QWPSR).

For those who haven't memorised all the Burgundy villages, this wine helpfully states it is from the Burgundy (Bourgogne) region.

Number of bottles produced (small).

Region of origin (single top-rated vineyard).

EU quality category (QWPSR).

Indicates that the wine comes from a top-rated (*Grand Cru*) vineyard.

Number of bottles produced (very small).

Two Côte d'Or Red Burgundies. The differences between these two labels are subtle, but reflect considerable differences in quality and price. Pinot Noir is the grape variety in both cases. However, while the grapes for the Gevrey-Chambertin may come from a number of vineyards – great, good and ordinary – surrounding that village, those for the Clos de Vougeot must all come from a single, top-rated (*Grand Cru*) vineyard.

Other Premium Pinot Noir Regions

New Zealand shows the greatest promise as a source of Pinot Noir wines to rival the best from Burgundy. These wines are generally more full-bodied, with lower acidity and more intense fruit than the wines from Burgundy. Spicy notes often accompany the red fruit flavours (cherry, strawberry). Martinborough and Central Otago make the ripest, most intense New Zealand Pinot Noirs. The variety is also grown in Marlborough, where a lighter style is made, and much of the fruit is used for sparkling wine.

Germany is an important producer of Pinot Noir (where it is known as Spätburgunder). The wines tend to be intensely fruity with very soft tannins.

Most of the regions in **California** are too hot for good quality Pinot Noir, but good examples can be found in Carneros and in cooler parts of Sonoma County such as the Russian River Valley. Californian Pinot Noirs tend to be full-bodied. Most are intensely fruity, but some display pronounced animal and vegetal characteristics (leather, meat, wet leaves). A suitably moderate climate is found further north in **Oregon**, where some very high-quality Pinot Noir wines are produced.

Most **Australian** regions are too hot for Pinot Noir, though some premium quality wines are being made in sites that benefit from the cooling effects of ocean breezes or altitude, such as the Yarra Valley.

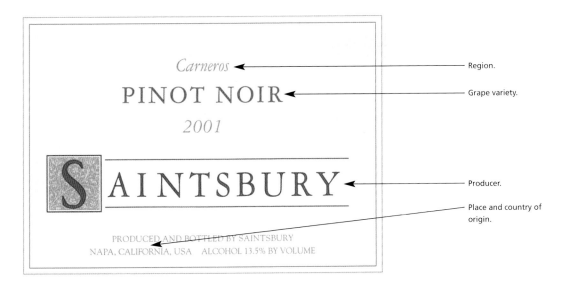

Carneros — Region.

PINOT NOIR — Grape variety.

2001

SAINTSBURY — Producer.

PRODUCED AND BOTTLED BY SAINTSBURY
NAPA, CALIFORNIA, USA   ALCOHOL 13.5% BY VOLUME — Place and country of origin.

The Casablanca Valley in **Chile** is emerging as a source of intensely fruity Pinot Noirs, often with flavours of strawberry jam.

South Africa also makes some high quality Pinot Noirs, in small quantities, from coastal sites.

BULK-PRODUCTION REGIONS FOR INEXPENSIVE PINOT NOIR

Because Pinot Noir is such a tricky grape to grow, there are few inexpensive sources. Many of the regions that produce large volumes of inexpensive varietal wines such as Central Valley (California), Riverina (Australia) and most of the Vin de Pays d'Oc are simply too hot for Pinot Noir. The main source of inexpensive Pinot Noir is **Romania**.

Romanian Pinot Noirs vary widely in style. Some are soft, light and strawberryish; others can have astringent tannins or taste of cooked fruits (prune, strawberry jam). **Chile** also produces some inexpensive Pinot Noir wines in a soft, fruity style.

PINOT NOIR IN BLENDS

Pinot Noir produces its finest still wines unblended (though it is used as a component of many sparkling wines, including most Champagne). The most commonly found blends are the basic Red Burgundies. These are blends of Pinot Noir with Gamay. Apart from a few obscure exceptions, a red wine labelled Bourgogne AC will be 100% Pinot Noir.

7 Cabernet Sauvignon and Merlot

These two grape varieties are often grown together and blended together. Merlot is often added to Cabernet Sauvignon to produce a wine that is more easily drinkable, as the Merlot supplies softness and body to an otherwise quite austere wine. Cabernet Sauvignon is often added to Merlot to add tannin, acidity and aromatic fruit. The classic region for such blends is Bordeaux, but it is common for a small amount of blending to occur in New World varietally labelled wines, even though this is not mentioned on the label.

THE FLAVOURS OF CABERNET SAUVIGNON

Cabernet Sauvignon is a black grape variety that gives deeply coloured wines that have lots of tannin and acidity, and strong aromas. Typical flavours include black fruits (blackcurrant, black cherry), often accompanied by vegetal notes (bell pepper, mint, cedar). Oak is frequently used to age the premium wines, softening the tannins and adding oaky flavours (smoke, vanilla, coffee). Cabernet Sauvignon needs a moderate or hot climate; it cannot ripen in cool climates or cool years. Wines made from under-ripe Cabernet Sauvignon can be very harsh and astringent with unpleasant herbaceous flavours. Wines from hot climates are fuller-bodied, with softer tannins, more black cherry fruit and a less herbaceous character.

Because of the intense fruit flavours, and high levels of tannin and acidity, Cabernet Sauvignon is a good variety for making wines that age well.

THE FLAVOURS OF MERLOT

Merlot is also a black grape variety. It gives wines that are less aromatic, with less intense flavours and lighter tannins and acidity than Cabernet Sauvignon, but generally with more body and higher alcohol. Flavours typically fall into one of two groups, depending on how ripe the grapes are. The common international style, made from grapes grown in hot climates or over-ripe grapes grown in moderate climates, shows a black fruit character (blackberry, black plum, black cherry), full body, medium or low acidity, high alcohol and medium levels of gentle tannins. Some super-ripe versions display fruitcake and chocolate flavours. Less common is a more elegant style, possible in moderate or cooler climates, showing a red fruit character (strawberry, red berry, plum), some vegetal notes (cedar), and a little more tannin and acidity. Like Cabernet Sauvignon, the best Merlot wines are often aged in oak, gaining spicy and oaky flavours (vanilla, coffee).

PREMIUM CABERNET SAUVIGNON AND MERLOT REGIONS
Bordeaux

Bordeaux is the classic home for these grape varieties. It has a moderate, maritime climate with long warm autumns that provide ideal conditions for Cabernet Sauvignon and Merlot. The region is based around the Gironde estuary in southwest France, where the Garonne and Dordogne rivers meet. For premium quality wines, it is helpful to focus on two zones within the Bordeaux region.

West and South of the Gironde and Garonne lies the zone many refer to as the Left Bank. Running from north to south, the main appellations here are the **Médoc**, **Haut-Médoc** (including the communes **Pauillac** and **Margaux**), and **Graves** (including the commune **Pessac-Léognan**). Here, Cabernet Sauvignon is the dominant variety. The

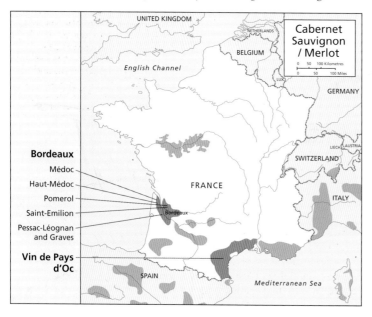

Premium Cabernet Sauvignon vineyard in Bordeaux. The gravelly soil helps store heat to aid ripening, and rapidly drains away excess water.

best sites are on gravel mounds that drain water away and retain heat to aid ripening. The wines are medium or full-bodied, with high levels of tannin and acidity, medium alcohol, and long length. They can be very tough when young, but with age the tannins soften, and flavours of black fruit (blackcurrant, black cherry) and toasty fragrant oak develop into vegetal, tobacco and cedar complexity. The very best wines come from the *Cru Classé* châteaux (see Chapter 11). Almost all of these are in the commune ACs. These are among the world's most complex and long-lived red wines.

The other major production zone for premium quality wines, the Right Bank, lies north and east of the Gironde and Dordogne. The most important appellations are **Saint-Emilion** and **Pomerol**. Merlot is the dominant variety here, and the wines are generally softer in style than those from the Left Bank. They typically have medium tannin levels, medium acidity, and a red fruit character (plum, red berry), developing cedar and tobacco notes as they age.

Many premium quality Bordeaux wines are made outside of the most prestigious appellations. These are labelled simply as **Bordeaux AC** or **Bordeaux**

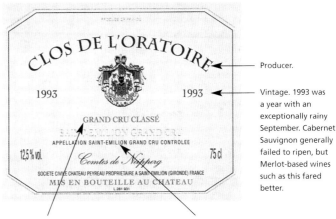

Producer.

Vintage. 1993 was a year with an exceptionally rainy September. Cabernet Sauvignon generally failed to ripen, but Merlot-based wines such as this fared better.

This estate is *Grand Cru Classé*, one of the top ranks for châteaux in Saint-Emilion.

The appellation (repeated). Unlike the Classed growth châteaux in the Haut Médoc, the *Grand Cru* classification is included in the appellation system in Saint-Emilion.

Supérieur AC. These medium-bodied dry reds generally have medium tannin levels and acidity, and a mixture of red and black fruit flavours from the Merlot and Cabernet Sauvignon components. They are generally best consumed while quite young, but some can benefit from bottle age.

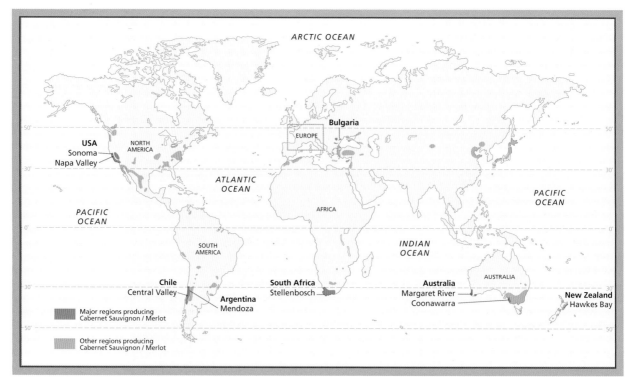

Other Premium Cabernet Sauvignon and Merlot Regions

Parts of **California**, particularly coastal counties such as Sonoma and parts of the Napa Valley, provide ideal conditions for Cabernet Sauvignon and Merlot. Premium Californian Cabernet Sauvignons typically have high levels of soft, ripe tannin, and are deeply coloured with black cherry

and oak flavours. Premium Californian Merlots are generally full-bodied, with soft black fruit and fruitcake and oak flavours. These two varieties also appear blended together, following the Bordeaux model.

Chile produces premium quality varietal and blended wines from Cabernet Sauvignon and Merlot. These often have pronounced vegetal characteristics (green bell pepper, blackcurrant leaf) accompanying intense black fruit flavours (black cherry, blackberry). The best regions are the Maipo Valley, close to Santiago, and parts of the Rapel Valley, further south. Due to previous confusion in the vineyards, some of the wine that is labelled as Merlot is in fact Carmenère, (an old, high quality variety, also originally from Bordeaux). This can add intense colour and spiced black fruit flavours (blackberry, liquorice, pepper).

In **Argentina**, Cabernet Sauvignon appears as varietal wines and blended with Malbec. Traditionally these wines were aged in oak for a long time before release, giving meaty, leathery flavours. Modern styles are more fruity.

Within the hot Mendoza region, where most of Argentina's exported wines are made, there are premium sites where climate is moderated by altitude. These are the source of the fruit for most of Argentina's best red wines.

Cabernet Sauvignon is widely grown in **Australia**, and two regions have established themselves as

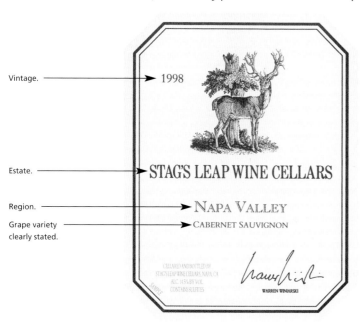

Vintage.

Estate.

Region.

Grape variety clearly stated.

modern classics. **Coonawarra** Cabernet often displays distinctive mint/eucalyptus flavours, accompanying the black fruit (black cherry) and oak notes (toast, vanilla). **Margaret River** in Western Australia produces varietal Cabernet Sauvignon and Cabernet-Merlot blends. These generally have high tannin levels, with black fruit and herb flavours (blackcurrant, blackcurrant leaf).

High quality Cabernet Sauvignons, Merlots and Cabernet-Merlot blends are made in the **Hawkes Bay** area of North Island, **New Zealand**. These typically have medium or high acidity and tannins, and herb aromas (cedar, blackcurrant leaf).

South Africa produces some very good Cabernet-Merlot blends, as well as pure varietal wines. These typically have less intense fruit and more herb flavours than similar wines from Australia or California. Many of the wines from **Stellenbosch** are close to the Bordeaux style, with high levels of tannin and acidity.

BULK-PRODUCTION REGIONS FOR INEXPENSIVE CABERNET SAUVIGNON AND MERLOT

Cabernet Sauvignon is a grape variety that can be cropped at quite high levels, in a range of climates (provided they are not too cool), and still retain some of its black fruit and high tannin character.

Chile (Central Valley) and **Southern France** (Vin de Pays d'Oc) produce large volumes of inexpensive, varietally expressive Cabernet Sauvignons, Merlots and Cabernet-Merlot blends. **South Africa** (Western Cape), **South Eastern Australia, California** (Central Valley), **Argentina** (Mendoza) and **Bulgaria** are also important areas, though they have more success with Cabernet Sauvignon than with Merlot. Many inexpensive Merlots are rather bland, though inoffensive – which could be why they are so popular. **Northern Italy** produces large volumes of inexpensive, light-bodied Merlot.

Much basic Bordeaux arguably comes under this heading. The best ones are soft, light or medium-bodied, and Merlot-based.

CABERNET SAUVIGNON AND MERLOT IN BLENDS

Cabernet Sauvignon and Merlot in blends together have already been described. In Australia, Shiraz is often used with Cabernet Sauvignon to give the softness and richness that Merlot supplies in Bordeaux and elsewhere. Merlot is sometimes blended with Malbec in Argentina, and Cabernet Sauvignon and Merlot are used with Carmenère in Chile. Cabernet Sauvignon is used in many regions to improve wines by adding a little aromatic fruit, colour and tannin.

8   Sauvignon Blanc

Some attribute the success of Sauvignon Blanc to its ability to create clear expectations (clean, crisp, refreshing, unoaked), and meet them. This is in contrast to Chardonnay, which is made in a very wide range of styles, and Riesling, which has failed to communicate its qualities to most wine consumers. We shall see, however, that Sauvignon is capable of more than one style.

THE FLAVOURS OF SAUVIGNON BLANC

Sauvignon Blanc is an aromatic white grape variety. Its wines usually display strong aromas of green fruit and vegetation (gooseberry, elderflower, green bell pepper, asparagus). They are usually high in acidity, medium-bodied, and almost always dry. In order to show its vegetal-aromatic character, Sauvignon Blanc needs a cool climate, though it will tolerate a moderate one. Wines from moderate regions, however, tend to lack the intense pungent vegetal complexity of wines from premium, cool-climate sites.

Most varietal Sauvignons have no oak flavours, because the style sought is one dominated by refreshing fruitiness. Those that are aged in oak generally come from moderate regions, and the oak can add flavours of toast and spice (vanilla, liquorice). Most varietal Sauvignons do not benefit from bottle age: although they may last, they lose their attractive freshness and rapidly become stale. Sauvignon Blanc, with its high levels of acidity, is also suitable for sweet wines, particularly in Sauternes (see Chapter 23).

PREMIUM SAUVIGNON BLANC REGIONS
Loire Central Vineyards

The villages of **Sancerre** and **Pouilly-Fumé** face each other across the Loire. The cool climate results in dry white wines with high acidity, medium body, with moderate or pronounced vegetal flavours. These wines are usually more restrained than Sauvignons from New Zealand, but still have varietal green fruit and herbaceous notes (gooseberry, grass, blackcurrant leaf, nettle), often with a hint of smokiness that many associate with the soils here, which in parts are similar to those of Chablis.

Bordeaux

Most premium white Bordeaux is a blend of Sémillon and Sauvignon Blanc, often with the Sémillon dominating. Sauvignon alone is usually a fruity wine, unsuited to ageing. Adding a proportion of Sémillon can help sustain the fruit character, and allows complexity to develop in the bottle. Sémillon wines generally add body to the blend too. Sémillon alone can be rather bland and neutral in youth, and adding a proportion of Sauvignon brings aromatic fruit character and refreshing acidity to the blend. These are dry wines, with medium or high acidity, medium or full body, sometimes with oaky flavours. The very best wines, such as those from *Cru Classé* châteaux in the Pessac-Léognan AC and the best white, Graves AC, age well and develop honeyed, toasty complex flavours in the bottle.

Other Premium Sauvignon Blanc Regions

Cool-climate Marlborough in South Island, **New Zealand**, has established itself as a new classic region for very expressive Sauvignon Blanc wines. There is an increasing range of styles as producers experiment and attempt to find a point of difference for their own wines, so some are more restrained, or show hints of oak or lees flavours,

UNITED KINGDOM

NETHERLANDS

BELGIUM

English Channel

LUX.

GERMANY

Sauvignon Blanc

0   50   100 Kilometres
0   50   100 Miles

LIECH.   AUSTRIA

SWITZERLAND

FRANCE

ITALY

Loire
Sancerre
Pouilly-Fumé

Bordeaux
Pessac-Léognan and Graves
Sauternes (sweet wines)

Vin de Pays d'Oc

SPAIN

Mediterranean Sea

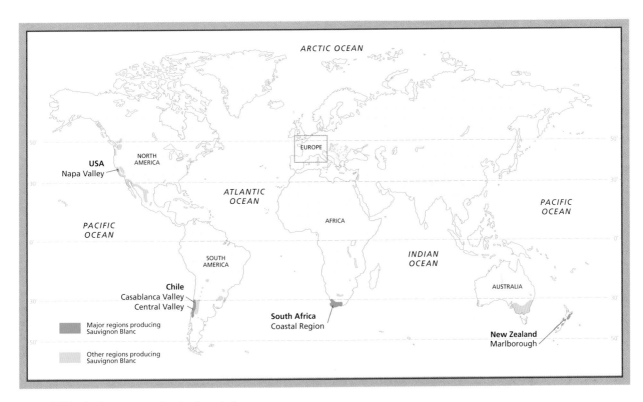

or are full-bodied. However, the classic style is dry, with high acidity, no oak, medium-bodied and characterised by intense, pungent, clean, varietal flavours (passion fruit, gooseberry, green pepper, blackcurrant leaf). These wines are best consumed while youthful and fresh, though some enjoy the vegetal (asparagus, pea) notes that develop in the bottle.

South Africa produces high quality Sauvignon Blancs in broadly two styles. Some are pungent and fruit driven, like those from New Zealand, but usually less intense and complex. Others use oak to make a wine that is less pungent, but can age in the bottle, gaining toasty complexity. These follow the Bordeaux model, but have a more intense, herbaceous varietal Sauvignon character.

In most parts of **California**, the conditions are too warm for the herbaceous characteristics of Sauvignon to be retained. Despite the climate, some interesting wines are made, especially in the Napa Valley, often labelled as Fumé Blanc. Depending on the producer, and the consumer the wine is made for, the style may be unoaked, lightly oaked or even heavily oaked. Compared to the oak-aged Chardonnays from the same region, the oaked Fumé Blancs are generally a little less full-bodied, and higher in acidity. Some of the vegetal varietal character of the Sauvignon Blanc (grass, asparagus) usually shines through the spicy, oaky flavours (toast, liquorice, vanilla).

Region of production. This allows you to deduce the grape variety: white Sancerre must be 100% Sauvignon Blanc.

EU quality category (QWPSR).

Chile is emerging as a source of vegetal, fruit-led premium Sauvignon Blanc, particularly from cooler regions such as the Casablanca Valley.

Machine harvesting of Sauvignon Blanc grapes in the vineyard of Cloudy Bay, Marlborough, New Zealand. This is an efficient method of harvesting grapes, allowing large areas of vineyard to be harvested quickly, when the grapes reach optimal ripeness.

Producer. ——————

Country of origin. ——————

Grape variety. ——————

Region in New Zealand renowned for Sauvignon Blanc.

BULK-PRODUCTION REGIONS FOR INEXPENSIVE SAUVIGNON BLANC

Outside of the premium Loire appellations, France produces large volumes of inexpensive Sauvignon Blanc. Some of this is AC wine (e.g. Touraine AC). Much basic white Bordeaux AC (mainly Sauvignon-Sémillon blends) is inexpensive, high-volume wine. Bordeaux is increasingly selling varietally labelled pure Sauvignon Blancs, often at low prices. Vin de Pays du Val de Loire and Vin de Pays d'Oc are also important sources of Sauvignon Blanc.

Chile, California and South Africa produce inexpensive varietal Sauvignons.

SAUVIGNON BLANC IN BLENDS

The most important blended wines with Sauvignon are dry white Bordeaux (see above) and Sauternes (see Chapter 23). Sauvignon Blanc/Semillon blends are also made in Australia, the USA and Chile.

Riesling

Riesling has a pronounced fruity, varietal character which is expressed in its wines wherever the grapes are grown, and whatever style (dry, medium, sweet) is made. However, different soil types and different ripeness levels emphasise different aspects of this varietal character. Because of its ability, like Chardonnay, to express the nuances of individual vineyard sites, it is common (especially in Germany, Alsace and Austria) for producers to bottle their wines with the name of the vineyard on the label.

9

THE FLAVOURS OF RIESLING

Riesling is an aromatic white grape variety. It is fruity and floral rather than vegetal like Sauvignon Blanc. In cool climates, if the fruit is harvested when ripe (rather than over-ripe), the wines have green fruit flavours (green apple, grape) with floral notes and sometimes a hint of citrus fruit (lemon, lime). In moderate regions, the citrus and stone fruit notes become dominant, and some wines can smell very strongly of fresh lime or white peach.

Because sugars build up slowly in this variety, and it retains its acidity well, Riesling is suitable for late-harvesting in regions where there are stable, dry, sunny autumn conditions. Stone fruit and tropical fruit notes can develop (peach, apricot, pineapple, mango). These late-harvest styles can be dry, medium or sweet in style. Riesling is very susceptible to noble rot, which concentrates sugars and acidity and makes this grape ideal for lusciously sweet wines (see Chapter 23).

High acidity levels and intense fruit help many Riesling wines to age in the bottle, where they develop flavours of honey and toast. Smoky petrol-like aromas sometimes appear in old Riesling wines. New oak is almost never used.

PREMIUM RIESLING REGIONS
Germany

Germany is the home of Riesling. Wines are made in a range of styles. Basic Rieslings will be classified as QbA (Qualitätswein bestimmter Anbaugebiete). These are usually fruity and refreshing, with medium sweetness. Above this in quality come the Prädikatswein. These vary in style according to their particular Prädikat.

Kabinett Rieslings are light in body, with high acidity and green fruit notes (apple, grape). They usually have medium sweetness and light alcohol, though they can be dry with medium alcohol.

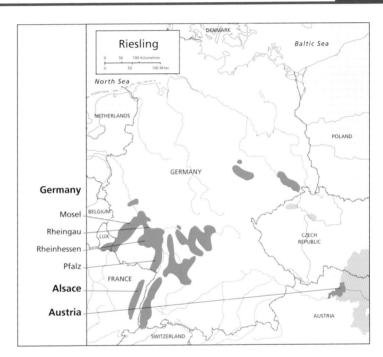

Compared to *Kabinett* wines, *Spätlese* (late harvest) Rieslings have a bit more body and citrus and exotic fruit notes (lemon, pineapple).

Auslese Rieslings have even more body and exotic fruit notes (pineapple, mango). This is the highest category to appear as a dry wine, though most Riesling *Auslese* wines are medium or sweet.

Beerenauslese and *Trockenbeerenauslese* Rieslings are sweet wines made from noble rot affected grapes (see Chapter 23).

Eiswein is a sweet wine made from frozen grapes (see Chapter 23).

Mosel produces Germany's lightest-bodied Rieslings. The *Kabinett* and *Spätlese* wines are almost always made with medium sweetness balanced by high acidity. The most prestigious vineyards are on very steep slopes surrounding the villages of Piesport and Bernkastel. **Rheingau**

Region.

Producer.

Vintage.
Name of an outstanding individual
vineyard near the village of Erbach.

Grape variety and Prädikat (see Chapter 12).

EU Quality Category: Prädikatswein is a QWPSR;
prior to 2007 these were labelled as
Qualitätswein mit Prädikat or QmP.

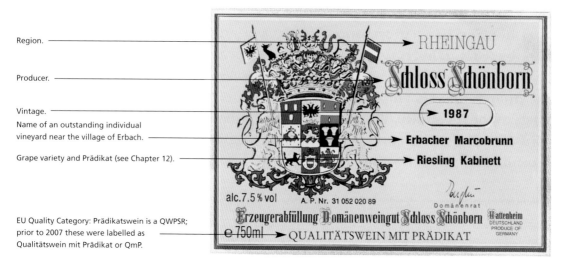

RHEINGAU

Schloss Schönborn

1987

Erbacher Marcobrunn

Riesling Kabinett

alc.7.5 % vol   A. P. Nr. 31 052 020 89
Domänenrat
Erzeugerabfüllung Domänenweingut Schloss Schönborn Hattenheim
DEUTSCHLAND
PRODUCE OF
GERMANY
e 750ml ➤ QUALITÄTSWEIN MIT PRÄDIKAT

Separating Riesling grapes with botrytis (noble rot) from those without in the Scharzhofberg vineyard of Egon Müller, Wiltingen, Germany (Saar). Depending on the level of rot, those in the small bucket may be used for *Beerenauslese* or *Trockenbeerenauslese*. The labour involved in this degree of selection means these wines are very expensive to produce.

is a smaller region. Its *Kabinett*, *Spätlese* and *Auslese* Riesling wines are usually drier in style and medium-bodied. **Pfalz** is a large, southerly region that lies close to Alsace. The Riesling wines from vineyards around Forst and Deidesheim are generally dry and medium-bodied.

Other Premium Riesling Regions

The long, dry, warm autumns in **Alsace** provide ideal conditions for dry, medium-bodied Rieslings, with green, citrus and stone fruit notes. Fuller-bodied, late harvest wines are also made there, with more intense flavours and sometimes a hint of sweetness. Alsace has a very complicated

geology, with a wide range of soil types. The characteristics of Riesling wines can differ markedly from one site to another, even when the same winemaking techniques are used. The best wines benefit greatly from bottle age, and can last for decades, developing a smoky, honeyed complexity, often with petrol-like aromas.

Austria also produces medium and full-bodied dry Rieslings with citrus and stone fruit flavours and medium or high acidity. Wines from certain vineyards can have smoky, mineral aromas.

Australia produces outstanding Rieslings, particularly in the **Clare Valley** and **Eden Valley Regions**. These are dry, medium-bodied, with high acidity and pronounced citrus fruit notes (lime, lemon). The wines age well, developing notes of honey and toast. Some wines rapidly develop smoky aromas that are similar to petrol.

New Zealand produces some very good quality Rieslings, mainly in the South Island. These are dry, with high acidity and intense green fruit and citrus flavours (apple, grape, lime). Most are best consumed young, but some develop attractive honey flavours with age.

BULK-PRODUCTION REGIONS FOR INEXPENSIVE RIESLING

Many of the Riesling vines in the bulk production regions in Germany have been replaced with other, higher-yielding varieties that are used in the inexpensive Liebfraumilch-style blends. Both in Germany and elsewhere, there is relatively little large volume inexpensive production of varietal Riesling, though inexpensive, branded fruity-dry German Rieslings are becoming increasingly important. Some Australian brands include a South Eastern Australia Riesling in their portfolio.

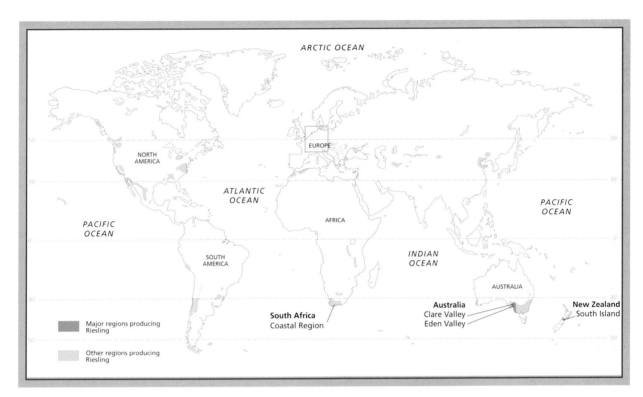

Much of the fruit for these will be sourced from premium areas such as the Eden or Clare Valleys, rather than the hot bulk-production regions further inland.

RIESLING IN BLENDS

For premium quality wines, Riesling is almost never blended. Little, if any, Riesling is used in the large volume, inexpensive German wines such as Liebfraumilch. In Australia, it is sometimes blended with the aromatic Gewurztraminer, to make fruity, quaffable, off-dry whites.

A NOTE ON VARIETAL LABELLING

Almost all Riesling wines are varietally labelled. It is worth pointing out that there are other varieties that have similar names. The most commonly encountered one is Welschriesling/ Laski Rizling/ Olaszrizling. This is a totally unrelated variety, widely grown in central and eastern Europe for crisp, light-bodied dry whites and a few luscious sweet wines.

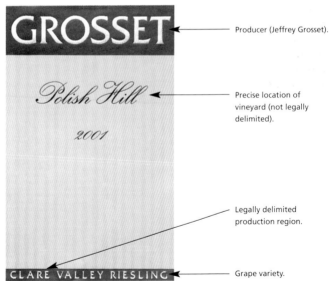

Producer (Jeffrey Grosset).

Precise location of vineyard (not legally delimited).

Legally delimited production region.

Grape variety.

This clean, simple label from Australia contrasts with the elaborate traditional label from Germany (above opposite). Many German estates are now using simpler labels.

10 Syrah and Grenache

The only country outside France to have established a sustained international reputation for premium quality Syrah (Shiraz) is Australia, though this is sure to change in the near future. Shiraz plantings are increasing in countries around the world, including South Africa, the USA, Chile and Argentina. Although Grenache is the third most widely planted black grape variety in terms of worldwide vineyard area, most of the vines are in Spain and southern France. It is most commonly used as part of a blend with other varieties.

THE FLAVOURS OF SYRAH/SHIRAZ

This black grape variety is known as Syrah in France and Shiraz in Australia. For simplicity, we will refer to it simply as Syrah.

Syrah grapes, like Cabernet Sauvignon, are small with thick, darkly coloured skins. The wines it makes are deeply coloured, with medium or high levels of tannins and acidity. The wines are usually full-bodied and generally have a black fruit (blackberry) and dark chocolate character. In wines from moderate regions, this may be accompanied by hints of herbaceousness (mint, eucalyptus), smoked meat, and spice (black pepper). In hot regions there are more sweet spice notes (liquorice, cloves). With age, the best wines develop animal and vegetal complexities (leather, wet leaves, earth). Syrah does not ripen in cool climates.

Many Syrah wines undergo some oak treatment, either through barrel ageing or the use of chips or staves. These can give toast, smoke, vanilla and coconut flavours to the wine.

THE FLAVOURS OF GRENACHE/GARNACHA

This black grape variety is known as Garnacha in Spain, but in most other regions it is known and appears on the wine label as Grenache.

Grenache grapes are large, with thin skins, high sugar levels and low acidity. The resulting wines are seldom deep in colour, but are usually very full-bodied. They typically have a red-fruit character (strawberry, raspberry), with spicy notes (white pepper, liquorice, cloves). With age, the spicy notes evolve into toffee and leather. Grenache needs a hot climate to ripen.

With their thin skins, it is easy to make rosé wines from Grenache grapes. These tend to be full-bodied and dry, with red fruit flavours (strawberry). Some are light-bodied and fruity, with medium sweetness.

Grenache is used widely for rosé wines in the southern Rhône, southern France and Spain. Most are best consumed while young and vibrant. Very few benefit from ageing, though some are aged in oak, which can give the wines an orange hue and dulls the fruit, but adds savoury complexity.

SYRAH AND GRENACHE TOGETHER

This combination works in a similar way to Cabernet Sauvignon and Merlot, though it is easier to make a complete, satisfying wine from Syrah than 100% Cabernet. Adding Grenache to Syrah can result in a wine with more alcohol, lower levels of tannin and acidity, and red fruit and extra spice flavours. Adding Syrah to a Grenache-based wine boosts the levels of colour, tannin and acidity, and adds a dark fruit character. Many southern Rhône wines include several other varieties, as well as Syrah and Grenache. Some of these (Mourvèdre and Cinsault) contribute to the character of the wine; others are used because they give high yields and are cheap or easy to grow.

South-facing vineyards on the hill of Hermitage give very full-bodied Syrah wines. The flatter vineyards to the east are entitled to the appellation Crozes-Hermitage AC.

In Australia, a Shiraz/Grenache blend is frequently a full-bodied, fruity red with very soft tannins, that is ideal for serving lightly chilled. There are also some more serious wines made from this combination, particularly from South Australia: full-bodied, intense and complex. These serious wines may include other varieties in the blend, such as Mataro (Mourvèdre). Such blends are known colloquially as 'GSMs'.

PREMIUM SYRAH AND GRENACHE REGIONS
The Northern Rhône

This is the classic region for Syrah wines. The finest wines are made from grapes grown on the steep terraces that tower above the Rhône. Many of these terraces are so narrow that no machinery can be used. The vineyard work has to be done by hand, which makes these wines expensive to produce. However, the sunlight and good drainage provide ideal conditions for the production of powerful, complex, ageworthy wines. The best appellations are **Côte-Rotie** and **Hermitage**, though these wines are rare and expensive. **Crozes-Hermitage** is a larger appellation that includes some flatter sites. Its wines are generally less intense and less complex than those of Côte-Rotie and Hermitage, but prices are lower. The wines often display the black pepper flavours, and tannins and acidity found in Syrah wines from a moderate climate.

The Southern Rhône

Here the valley broadens out and there are no steep slopes. The vineyards stretch far away from the Rhône, covering wide, stony plains. It is hotter and drier here than in the northern Rhône, and the conditions are ideal for Grenache. This is usually blended with other varieties such as Syrah, Mourvèdre and Cinsault.

The main regional appellation is **Côtes du Rhône**. Within this, the better vineyard sites are entitled to label their wines **Côtes du Rhône Villages**. Because of the possibilities available in terms of yields, choice of grape varieties in the blend, and winemaking techniques, styles and quality vary considerably. The very cheapest wines tend to be medium-bodied, with light tannins and a simple juicy red fruit and peppery-spice character. The best could pass for Châteauneuf-du-Pape in terms of body, complexity, intensity and length.

A number of communes in the southern Rhône have their own appellation, of which the most famous is **Châteauneuf-du-Pape**. Some wines are 100 per cent Grenache; most add some Syrah, Mourvèdre and Cinsault; very few use all of the

13 permitted varieties. Typical Châteauneuf-du-Pape is full-bodied, with medium tannins and low acidity and an intense, complex character that includes red fruit (strawberry), spice (pepper, liquorice), and animal (leather) notes.

Other Premium Regions for Syrah and Grenache

Australia is famed for its Shiraz (Syrah). Compared to the Syrah-based wines from the northern Rhône, Australian Shiraz is generally fuller-bodied, with softer tannins and less acidity. Due to the hot climates of many of the premium Shiraz regions, the flavours include intense black fruit (blackberry, plum), sweet spices and notes of black chocolate. Use of oak is often more overt in Australia than it is in France, giving smoke, vanilla and coconut flavours to many of the wines. Shiraz is grown widely in Australia, and many regional names can be seen on the wines.

A tractor working a vineyard in the southern Rhône. Stony soils such as these are common in many of the best sites: they store the heat of the day and radiate it out at night, helping the grapes achieve high ripeness and sugar levels.

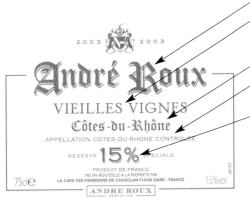

Producer.

Old vines. These often give low yields of very concentrated juice.

Region of production.

EU quality category (QWPSR).

Alcohol by volume. Stated very prominently for this wine! 2003 was an exceptionally hot year across much of Europe, and sugar levels in Grenache were particularly high.

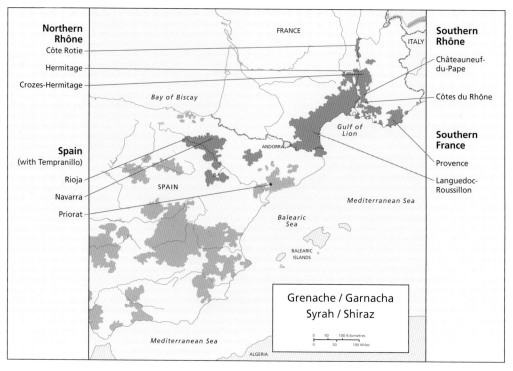

The most famous of these include the **Hunter Valley, McLaren Vale**, and the **Barossa Valley**. Shiraz from the Barossa is particularly powerful. The hot conditions there are also ideal for Grenache, though this is less commonly seen.

More moderate conditions are found in **Western Australia, Coonawarra**, and the mountainous parts of **Central** and **Western Victoria**. Shiraz from these regions is more peppery and less full-bodied than that from the hotter regions.

It is common to blend across regions. This allows Shiraz wines with different characteristics to be blended together to make a more complex whole. It also helps the production of premium wines of consistent quality and style in larger quantities. The multi-regional blends sometimes mention the origin of their constituents on the label, but more commonly say South Australia or even South Eastern Australia, though the latter is more likely to indicate an inexpensive wine where the majority is sourced from bulk production regions (see below).

Garnacha (Grenache) is the most widely planted variety in **Spain**, but although there are tiny quantities of some very high quality wines that sell at high prices, the majority is used for inexpensive, high-volume wines. It can be used as part of the blend (with Tempranillo and other varieties) in Rioja, though it is rarely dominant in the best wines from this region. Some of the finest (and most expensive) Grenache-based wines come from **Priorat**. Here, it is usually blended with Carignan and sometimes with other varieties including Cabernet Sauvignon and Syrah. The wines are deep-coloured, full-bodied and very intense. Garnacha is used widely for rosé wines in Spain – the best examples come from Navarra.

BULK-PRODUCTION REGIONS FOR INEXPENSIVE SYRAH AND GRENACHE

Much wine under the Côtes du Rhône appellation is made in large volumes to be sold at low prices. Grenache and Syrah are widely grown for use in appellation wines in Provence, Languedoc and Roussillon. As in the Southern Rhône, these wines are made from a blend of varieties. For appellations such as **Minervois, Corbières, Fitou, Côtes du Roussillon**, and **Languedoc**, the main

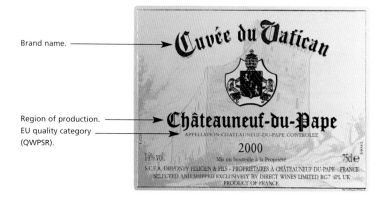

Brand name.

Region of production.
EU quality category (QWPSR).

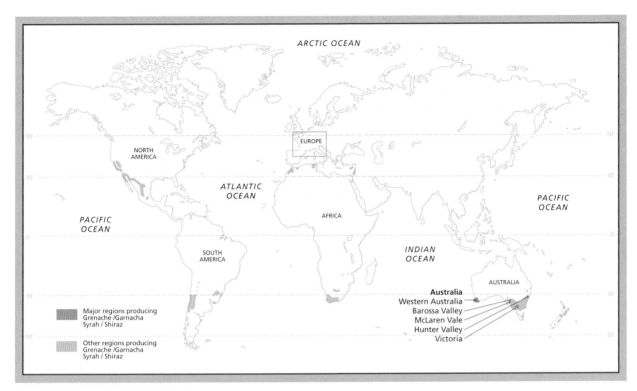

varieties in the blend are often Grenache and Carignan (the latter can give tough wines with high levels of acid and tannin). Syrah and Mourvèdre are used to improve the character of the better wines. Large quantities of inexpensive Grenache-led wines are also made in **Spain**.

For inexpensive Shiraz, the main production areas are Riverland, Murray-Darling and Riverina in Australia. (These names do not appear on labels; the wine will be labelled as **South Eastern Australia**.) There are also some inexpensive Vins de Pays Syrahs from the south of France.

SYRAH AND GRENACHE IN BLENDS

An increasingly fashionable combination is **Shiraz-Viognier** (strictly speaking this is not a blend, because the two varieties are fermented together, rather than blending their wines together). This follows a northern Rhône tradition of adding some white grapes to the fermentation of Syrah. Viognier helps give the wine a smooth texture, and adds a trace of exotic fruit character.

Syrah blended with Cabernet Sauvignon is

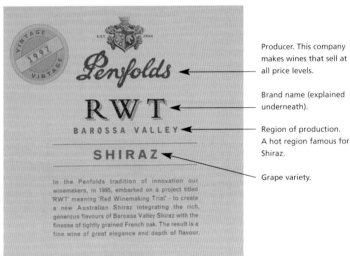

Producer. This company makes wines that sell at all price levels.

Brand name (explained underneath).

Region of production. A hot region famous for Shiraz.

Grape variety.

described in Chapter 7. Grenache blended with Syrah, Mourvèdre and Cinsault is covered in this chapter. Grenache blended with Tempranillo is covered in Chapter 14.

11 France

The classic grape varieties of France's greatest regions are now widely established in many other regions of the world. For this reason, the styles of many of the wines listed below are described in the preceding grape variety chapters. However, French laws covering the use of AC (Appellation Contrôlée) names rarely permit the naming of grape varieties. This can mean that, for example, fans of Chardonnay may not realise that some of the finest expressions of this variety come in bottles labelled as Chablis AC or Meursault AC. The most commonly encountered appellations for the classic varieties are listed below. In addition, wines from other regions, such as Anjou-Saumur and Touraine, and Alsace, whose grape varieties are not yet so well established in international vineyards, are described here.

BORDEAUX

The main form of branding for premium quality Bordeaux wines is the **château**. Names of merchant houses are sometimes used, but this is mainly for large-volume inexpensive wines. A château name does not necessarily refer to a grand building. It indicates that the wine has been made from a defined piece of land, rather than being assembled from bought-in wines, or made from bought-in grapes or juice. Over time, châteaux can sell or buy land, so the exact plots associated with the château name can change. The term **Grand Vin** is often used to indicate the main wine made by the Château, no matter how 'grand' or 'humble' the wine or the château. For more details about the styles of Bordeaux wines see Chapters 7, 8 and 23. The main appellations and labelling terms are:

Regional
Bordeaux AC: red and dry white wines
Claret: an English term for red Bordeaux wines
Bordeaux Supérieur AC: a designation that requires a higher level of alcohol than basic Bordeaux AC

Médoc (red wines only)
Médoc AC
Haut-Médoc AC
Pauillac AC
Margaux AC
Cru Bourgeois: a rank of château in the Médoc, of good quality but generally not as good as *(Grand) Cru Classé*: one of the châteaux judged to be of the finest quality in 1855. This classification is still relevant as an indicator of quality.

Graves (red and dry white wines)
Graves AC
Pessac-Léognan AC: a superior part of Graves
Cru Classé: the best châteaux (all lie within the Pessac-Léognan AC)

Saint-Emilion (red wines only)
Saint-Emilion AC
Saint-Emilion *Grand Cru* AC: a wine of superior quality

Pomerol (red wines only)
Pomerol AC

Producer. In Bordeaux a château refers to a specified plot of land, though parts of this plot may be sold or added to over time. The name of the château can also be changed, as this was in 1989 from Château Mouton-Baronne-Philippe.

1989 was an outstanding vintage. A warm dry ripening season led to flavourful wines with high levels of soft ripe tannins.

This château was judged to be a 5th growth in 1855, putting it just within the top 60 or so châteaux in the region.

Commune (production region) and EU quality category (QWPSR).

Château d'Armailhac
1989
Grand Cru Classé
PAUILLAC

MIS EN BOUTEILLE AU CHATEAU   12.5 % vol.

BURGUNDY

Wines from the wider Burgundy region are
labelled as Bourgogne AC. The best wines come
from the Côte d'Or, which is split into the Côte de
Nuits to the north and the Côte de Beaune to the
south. These wines are generally labelled with the
name of the village (e.g. Nuits-Saint-Georges AC)
and the grape variety is rarely mentioned. Vines in
neighbouring vineyards with subtly different soils
or topography can produce wines in surprisingly
different styles and quality levels, which may sell
at vastly differing prices, and these differences are
incorporated into the appellation system. Within a
village, the better vineyard sites have *Premier Cru*
status, and the very best are designated *Grand Crus*.

In Burgundy, and elsewhere in France, a **domaine**
is a producer that makes wine exclusively from
grapes grown in their own vineyards. They do not
buy in grapes, juice, or finished wines to sell under
their own name. For more detail about the styles
of Burgundy wines see Chapters 5 and 6. The
main appellations and labelling terms are:

Regional
Bourgogne AC: red or white wines

Red Burgundy

Côte d'Or
Gevrey-Chambertin AC
Nuits-Saint-Georges AC
Beaune AC
Pommard AC

White Burgundy

Chablis
Chablis AC
Chablis *Premier Cru* AC: wine from a better
vineyard
Chablis *Grand Cru* AC: a wine from the very
best vineyards

Côte d'Or
Puligny-Montrachet AC
Meursault AC

Mâconnais
Mâcon AC
Mâcon-Villages AC: a wine from superior sites
within the Mâconnais
Pouilly-Fuissé AC

BEAUJOLAIS

Light and medium-bodied red wines are produced
here from the **Gamay** grape variety. These are
usually unoaked and have medium or high acidity,
low tannin levels and pronounced red fruit aromas
(raspberry, cherry), sometimes with a hint of spice

Individually staked Gamay
vines in Beaujolais.

Production region and
EU quality category
(QWPSR). Beaujolais-
Villages is a region of
granite hills within the
wider Beaujolais region.
It produces wines that
are generally higher in
quality, with more
concentration and
character than ordinary
Beaujolais.

Producer. A domaine is
a producer that makes
wines from their own
vineyards, rather than
buying in grapes, juice
or wines.

(cinnamon, pepper). They are best consumed
while young and fruity, though a few wines from
Morgon AC and Moulin-à-Vent AC can improve
with bottle-age.

Beaujolais AC
Beaujolais Nouveau AC: a very light style of
Beaujolais released in the November following
the harvest
Beaujolais Villages AC: superior quality wines
that come from the granite hills to the north of
the region

Within the Beaujolais Villages AC, there are ten
villages, known as the Beaujolais *Crus*, which
produce the best quality wines from the
Beaujolais region. These label their wine with

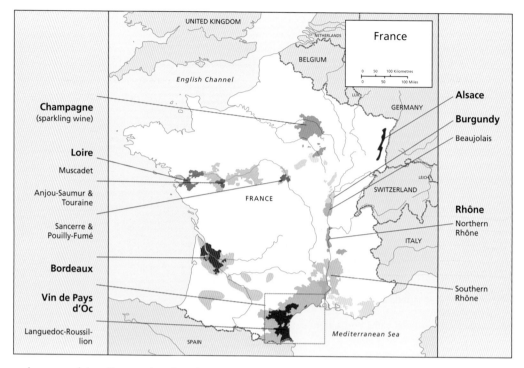

the name of the village, rather than the region. The most commonly seen ones are Fleurie AC, Brouilly AC, Morgon AC and Moulin-à-Vent AC.

ALSACE
The Vosges mountains to the west of Alsace shelter the region from rain-bearing winds blowing across northern France. Vines are planted on the eastern foothills, and benefit from the morning sun. The name of the grape variety usually appears on the label, along with the appellation:

Alsace AC
Alsace *Grand Cru* AC: a wine from a superior vineyard site

Styles of **Riesling** wines are described in Chapter 9.

Although **Pinot Gris** is the same grape variety as Pinot Grigio (see Chapter 13), the style of wine made in Alsace is very different. Here Pinot Gris is used for full-bodied dry, medium and sweet white wines with spicy tropical fruit flavours (ginger, banana, melon), sometimes with hints of honey.

Gewurztraminer gives intensely perfumed white wines, that can be dry, off-dry, or medium in style, and full-bodied, with high alcohol. Typical flavours include floral perfume (rose, orange blossom), tropical and stone fruit (lychee, peach,

grape), and musky sweet spices (ginger, cinnamon). Most are best consumed while they are youthful and freshly fruity, but some develop interesting meat, honey and nut aromas with age.

Refreshing, unoaked, white wines are also made from Pinot Blanc and Muscat. These wines are usually dry. Although most Alsace wines are white, some very light reds are made from Pinot Noir.

THE LOIRE VALLEY   WEST COAST
The Central Vineyards
For more details, see Chapter 8. The main appellations are:

Sancerre AC
Pouilly-Fumé AC

Touraine and Anjou-Saumur (white)
The **Chenin Blanc** grape variety is used for white wines in a range of styles. Most are medium-bodied wines, with medium sweetness, high acidity, unoaked, with citrus, green and tropical fruit notes (lemon, apple, pineapple), and some vegetal aromas (green leaf). Dry and sweet whites are also made. Chenin Blanc, like Riesling, Pinot Gris and Sémillon, is very susceptible to noble rot (see Chapter 23). The main appellations are:

Vouvray AC: premium appellation for Chenin Blanc (dry, medium or sweet)

Touraine AC: inexpensive dry whites made from Sauvignon Blanc or Chenin Blanc Saumur AC: premium and bulk/inexpensive whites from Chenin Blanc (dry, medium or sweet) Coteaux du Layon AC: sweet Chenin Blanc (see Chapter 23)

Touraine and Anjou-Saumur (rosé)

Medium and sweet rosés appear under the following ACs:

Rosé d'Anjou AC
Cabernet d'Anjou AC

Touraine and Anjou-Saumur (red)

Cabernet Franc is used for medium and light-bodied red wines, usually with high acidity, light or medium tannins and red fruit and vegetal flavours (redcurrant, raspberry, cedar, green pepper). The main appellations are:

Chinon AC
Bourgueil AC

The Nantais

Medium-bodied, dry, unoaked white wines with light, almost neutral fruit and medium or high acidity are made from **Muscadet**, a white grape variety.

Muscadet AC
Muscadet-Sèvre et Maine AC: a large subregion, producing superior wines
Sur lie: the wine has been bottled from a vessel containing the dead yeast left over from fermentation. These give a little more body and complexity to the wine.

THE RHÔNE VALLEY

For more details about the styles of these wines see Chapter 10. The main appellations and labelling terms are:

Northern Rhône
Crozes-Hermitage AC
Hermitage AC
Côte-Rotie AC

Southern Rhône
Châteauneuf-du-Pape AC
Côtes du Rhône AC
Côtes du Rhône Villages AC: superior subregion of Côtes du Rhône, offering wines with more intensity, complexity and length.

Vintage. Muscadet is generally best consumed as young as possible.

Producer.

Sur lie indicates that the wine has been bottled directly from a vessel containing the dead yeast sediment (lees) left over from fermentation. It gives a little yeasty character, body and a slight spritz to the wine.

Region of production and EU quality category.

Old vines.

LANGUEDOC-ROUSSILLON

The majority of France's *Vin de Pays* wines are produced here (**Vin de Pays d'Oc**), but there are also some important AC wines. Most of these are red, made from a blend of local grape varieties that usually includes Grenache and, increasingly, Syrah. Style and quality vary greatly. Those with a large Grenache component are full-bodied, with red fruit and spice flavours. Although a few premium quality, high-price wines are produced in these appellations, the majority are inexpensive, straightforward wines.

Languedoc AC
Minervois AC
Corbières AC
Fitou AC
Côtes du Roussillon AC

VINS DE PAYS

These produce large quantities of inexpensive wines from international grape varieties such as Chardonnay, Sauvignon Blanc, Cabernet Sauvignon, Merlot and Syrah. The variety or blend is usually stated on the label. Where no varieties are mentioned, the wine is more likely to be made from lesser-known, local grape varieties. The main southern Vin de Pays is Vin de Pays d'Oc. Large volumes of inexpensive Sauvignon Blanc, Chenin Blanc and Chardonnay are sold as Vin de Pays du Val de loire. This designation covers the whole of the Loire Valley.

12 Germany

Traditional German wine labels often have a profusion of information, which can appear confusing at first. The detail frequently includes the village and individual vineyard from which the grapes came, for example, Piesporter Goldtröpchen (Piesport is the village, Goldtröpchen is a single premium-site vineyard that towers steeply above Piesport). Alternatively, a village and a group of vineyards may be named, for instance, Piesporter Michelsberg (Michelsberg is a large group of vineyards including many non-premium sites several kilometres from Piesport). Unfortunately, there is no easy way to distinguish from the label whether the named site is a premium single vineyard or a large group of sites with lower quality potential. Most of the better wines are varietally labelled and give information about the style category (Prädikat).

GERMAN LABELLING TERMS: QUALITY AND STYLE

Although a few wines from non-traditional varieties appear under the basic *Deutscher Tafelwein* and *Landwein* quality categories (see Chapter 4), the most important quality wines are labelled as QbA (*Qualitätswein bestimmter Anbaugebiete*) or *Prädikatswein*. Within the *Prädikatswein* category, there is a hierarchy of designations that reflect the sugar content of the grapes that are used to make the wine. In order of increasing ripeness, they are:

> Kabinett
> Spätlese
> Auslese
> BA (Beerenauslese) and Eiswein
> TBA (Trockenbeerenauslese)

These categories can apply to all grape varieties, though the best examples are made with Riesling. More detail on the styles of these wines can be found in Chapters 9 and 23.

The terms **Grosses Gewächs**, **Erstes Gewächs** and **Erste Lage** indicate high quality dry wines from a single named vineyard. **Classic** and **Selection** also indicate a dry wine.

All of these must be varietally labelled.

Producer.

Bottled at the estate.

Prädikat (style category).

Grape variety.

Vintage.

Individual vineyard name.

Village.

EU Quality Category: Prädikatswein is a QWPSR; prior to 2007 these were labelled as Qualitätswein mit Prädikat or QmP.

Region of Production: Mosel (known as Mosel-Saar-Ruwer until 2007).

Gutsabfüllung

Schloss Saarstein

-54455 Serrig/Saar

V D P

1997 Riesling Spätlese
Serriger Schloss Saarsteiner

Qualitätswein mit Prädikat   A. P. Nr. 3 555 014-10-98

750 ml   Produce of Germany   alc. 8.0% by Vol.

MOSEL·SAAR·RUWER

MAIN PREMIUM QUALITY REGIONS

Germany is divided into 13 Quality Regions (*Anbaugebiete*), of which the most important for premium quality Riesling wines are Mosel, Rheingau and Pfalz (see Chapter 9).

BULK/INEXPENSIVE PRODUCTION WINES

Many premium quality German Riesling wines sell at surprisingly low prices. In addition, large-volume production inexpensive wines are made from other, lower-quality, higher-yielding grape varieties such as Müller-Thurgau, Silvaner and a number of varieties that have been specifically developed to

have very perfumed fruit and high sugar levels, in spite of the cool climate. These wines are usually very fruity and floral, with light body, medium sweetness, and medium or high acidity. They lack the character and refreshing crispness of Riesling wines from premium sites. The main production areas for these are Rheinhessen and Pfalz and many are labelled as **Liebfraumilch**, though use of this label term is declining as it is replaced by brands. It is a QbA with medium sweetness, made from a blend of grape varieties. A wine labelled as 'Hock' is similar in style to Liebfraumilch, but does not have to be a QbA.

Autumnal Riesling vines in the Goldtröpchen vineyard above Piesport, Germany (Mosel). This spectacular south-facing slope provides ideal conditions for ripening Riesling grapes. The flat sites on the other side of the river supply grapes for Piesporter Michelsberg.

13 Italy

Italy has a very large number of delimited wine regions. Many of these are small and obscure. Even if you can memorise where they all are, you will find that in many regions, the number of permitted grape varieties is large, and a diverse range of styles and quality levels is produced. Because of this, some Italian wine labels can be of little help when it comes to deducing what the wine will be like, without detailed knowledge of the producer. Fortunately, many other labels name the grape variety used (Sangiovese di Toscana, Montepulciano d'Abruzzo, Primitivo di Puglia, Barbera d'Alba, Trentino Pinot Grigio, for example). In addition, understanding the styles of the major, traditional regions is a very good starting point for understanding the wines from other regions that use the same grape varieties.

ITALIAN LABELLING TERMS

Classico: indicates the historic core of many DOC regions. Usually these are the best sites, and produce the best wines.

Riserva: indicates that a DOC wine has been aged in barrel and bottle for a certain minimum period, set in law.

RED WINE REGIONS AND GRAPE VARIETIES
Premium Wines

The most famous wines from Piemonte (northwest Italy) are **Barolo DOCG** and **Barbaresco DOCG**. These are made from the **Nebbiolo** grape, which gives full-bodied wines with high tannins, alcohol and acidity. Red fruit flavours are accompanied by floral and earthy notes (strawberry, rose, tar), which with age can evolve into vegetal and animal components (mushroom, meat, leather). Piemonte also produces wines from the **Barbera** variety. These have light tannins, but high acidity and red fruit flavours (sour cherry). Most are unoaked, but some have toast and vanilla flavours from a period in oak.

In northeast Italy, the main region for red wines is **Valpolicella (Classico) DOC**. These are made with a blend of grapes, of which the main one is **Corvina**. The wines range considerably in style. Many fall under the bulk, inexpensive category, and are generally light in body, colour, flavour and tannins, with medium or high acidity and red fruit flavours (sour cherry). The more expensive wines (usually from the Classico subregion) have more concentrated, complex flavours that can hint at cooked fruits (baked plum, dried cherries).

In central Italy, the most important classic red is **Chianti** in Tuscany. This is made from a blend of varieties, with **Sangiovese** dominating. These medium-bodied reds have high levels of tannin and acidity, and red fruit flavours (sour cherry, red plum) often accompanied by dusty, earthy notes. As with Valpolicella, much basic Chianti is inexpensive, bulk production wine, with the better wines usually coming from the subregions such as **Chianti Classico DOCG** and **Chianti Ruffina DOCG**.

Abruzzo is a region in east-central Italy. **Montepulciano d'Abruzzo DOC** is a medium-bodied red wine made from the **Montepulciano** grape variety. The wines are deeply coloured, with medium acidity and tannins and red fruit flavours (plum, cherry), sometimes with hints of bitter coffee. (This should not be confused with Vino Nobile di Montepulciano, which is a Chianti-style red wine made with Sangiovese from the Tuscan town of Montepulciano.)

Producer.

Production region and EU quality category (QWPSR). *Classico* indicates the historic core of the Chianti region, where the best vineyard sites are located and the best wines made. This wine actually comes from the 'Conca d'Oro', or Golden Shell near Panzano, a site that is particularly suited to Sangiovese.

Vintage. Riserva indicates that the wine has been aged in oak for a minimum period, set by Italian law. This extended oak ageing is usually only used for the best wines.

Villa Cafaggio
Chianti Classico
Denominazione di Origine Controllata e Garantita
Riserva 1999
Panzano in Chianti

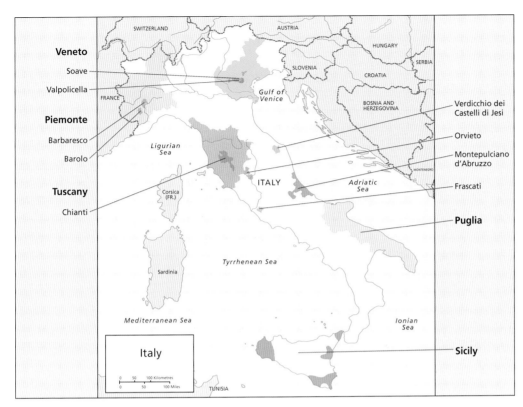

Southern Italy is producing increasing quantities of high quality red wines, under a profusion of different DOCs from a range of local and 'foreign' grape varieties. The most important local varieties are **Primitivo** and **Negroamaro** (in Puglia) and **Aglianico** (in Campania and Basilicata). These all produce deeply coloured, intensely flavoured red wines with high levels of tannin and acidity. Bitter flavours (coffee, dark chocolate) often accompany red, black and dried fruit notes (cherry, blackberry, prune). Primitivo wines are often very high in alcohol. It is the same variety as Zinfandel (see Chapter 19).

As well as producing large volumes of anonymous bulk inexpensive wines, **Sicily** is a source of some high-quality wines from Italian and international grape varieties. These are sometimes blended together.

Bulk/Inexpensive Wines

The main region for high-volume inexpensive red wines, in addition to Valpolicella and Chianti (described above) is southern Italy. Much of this is sold as non-vintage *Vino da Tavola*, with no region of origin on the bottle. Some name grape varieties, which could be Italian ones such as Primitivo, Negroamaro, or Sangiovese, or international ones such as Cabernet Sauvignon, Syrah or Merlot. It is quite common for these varieties to be blended together, which can help produce a balanced, attractive wine in large volumes from varieties which on their own might give wines that have excess or insufficient tannin, alcohol, acidity, fruit character or bitterness.

WHITE WINE VARIETIES AND REGIONS

Pinot Grigio (Pinot Gris) appears in a number of regions, though the best wines come from northeast Italy (Trentino, Veneto, Friuli). A typical Italian Pinot Grigio is dry, medium or light in body, with high acidity, and unoaked with delicate citrus and green fruit flavours (green apple, lemon). Most are quite simple wines, though some producers are making wines with more

Bunches of Nebbiolo grapes ripening in Barolo.

Part of the 'Golden Shell of Panzano' below Panzano in Chianti, Tuscany, Italy. These rolling hills provide some of the best locations for Sangiovese within the Chianti Classico DOCG region.

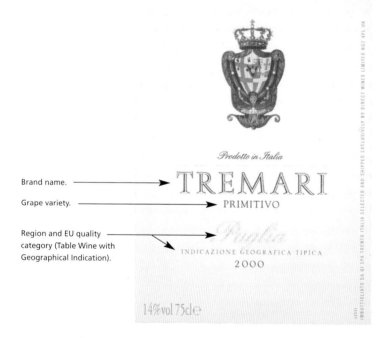

Brand name.

Grape variety.

Region and EU quality category (Table Wine with Geographical Indication).

Prodotto in Italia

TREMARI

PRIMITIVO

Puglia

INDICAZIONE GEOGRAFICA TIPICA

2000

14%vol 75cl

body, intensity and complexity, and riper flavours that include hints of melon and honey.

Other international grape varieties, such as Chardonnay, are grown throughout Italy. **Pinot Bianco** (Pinot Blanc) is grown particularly in the northeast, making white wines that are similar in style to an unoaked Chardonnay.

Verdicchio is a high-acid variety used for medium-bodied, crisp dry whites with lemon, herb (fennel) and bitter almond flavours. Most comes from the Verdicchio dei Castelli di Jesi DOC, near the east coast.

The most important traditional Italian whites, in terms of volume, are **Soave, Frascati** and **Orvieto**. Trebbiano grapes (the same as Ugni Blanc, distilled to make Cognac and Armagnac in France) supplies the bulk for the cheapest versions of all of these, and the resulting wines are dry, light-bodied, with medium acidity and rather neutral flavours. At higher prices, more characterful versions of all these wines exist. They generally contain a much higher proportion of high-quality local white grape varieties such as Garganega (Soave), Malvasia (Frascati) and Grechetto (Orvieto). Good quality Soave and Orvieto is crisp and refreshing. Good quality Frascati is more full-bodied.

Spain

Throughout Spain, it has been traditional to age wines for long periods in oak barrels, and then in bottle before release. This means that at any time, the vintages being released by Spanish producers are often older than those from other countries, even for inexpensive wines.

14

SPANISH LABELLING TERMS: QUALITY AND STYLE

Spanish law sets minimum periods of ageing in barrel and bottle for each of the following, but because these vary from one region to another, and are often exceeded by producers, the most important thing is to remember the order they come in. In order of increasing age, they are:

> Crianza
> Reserva
> Gran Reserva

Gran Reserva reds can sometimes be quite pale and garnet in colour, and the best are very complex wines. Putting an inferior wine through the long ageing process results in wines that are tired, stale, and lacking fruit. It is becoming more common to release wines while they are youthful and fruity. (**Joven** indicates a wine that has not been aged in oak.)

PREMIUM RED WINE REGIONS

The most important region for premium Spanish reds is **Rioja DOCa**. The main grape for this region is Tempranillo. This gives full or medium-bodied reds, with medium acidity, medium tannins and red fruit flavours (strawberry). It is often blended with Garnacha (Grenache), which can be the dominant variety in inexpensive Riojas. Grenache supplies high alcohol, and some spicy notes, with light tannins (see Chapter 10).

Much of the character of traditional-style Riojas comes from the oak ageing. This softens the tannins, and gives sweet coconut and vanilla flavours to the wine. Over time, some very savoury animal and vegetal flavours can develop (meat, leather, mushroom), particularly in the *Gran Reserva* wines.

Ribera del Duero DO also produces premium quality red wines from Tempranillo, with black fruit notes (blackberry, plum), and toasty oak flavours. In **Navarra DO**, Tempranillo is often blended with international grape varieties such as Merlot and Cabernet Sauvignon. Good quality reds are made in a range of styles in **Catalunya**, using Tempranillo, Garnacha and international grape varieties.

13,5% VOL.   75 Cl e

CINCO GENERACIONES
ELABORANDO VINO DE CALIDAD → Five generations making quality wine!

MARTINEZ BUJANDA ← Producer.

GRAN RESERVA ← Age statement. This indicates that the wine has spent a long period of ageing in barrel and bottle before release.

EMBOTELLADO POR
BODEGAS
MARTINEZ BUJANDA, S.A.
— OYON —
ESPAÑA

RIOJA ← Region and EU quality category (QWPSR).
DENOMINACION DE ORIGEN CALIFICADA
— PRODUCT —
OF SPAIN

SELECTED 16TH OCTOBER 2002

CUVÉE 4

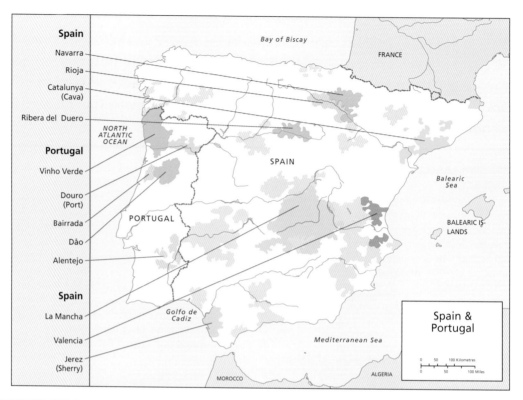

Freestanding Tempranillo vines in the chalky soils of Ribera del Duero.

PREMIUM WHITE WINE REGIONS

Spain also produces many interesting white wines. Modern-style whites from Rias Baixas and Rueda are fruity, with refreshing acidity. A wide range of styles is produced in Catalunya, from local as well as international grape varieties such as Chardonnay. Traditional white Rioja is full-bodied with nutty, oaky flavours, though unoaked styles are also made.

BULK/INEXPENSIVE PRODUCTION REGIONS

Tempranillo and Garnacha are grown throughout Spain, and the oak-aging techniques used in Rioja are widely adopted. There are many regions producing wine in a similar style to Rioja (soft tannins, strawberry fruit, oak flavours), but usually with less intensity or complexity. These regions include **La Mancha DO** and **Valdepeñas DO**. **Valencia DO** produces large quantities of inexpensive wines in all styles (red, white, rosé, dry, medium, sweet).

Portugal

In Portugal there has been a long tradition of blending across regions, and selling wines under brand names. The best regions for non-fortified dry wines are still being discovered, and the best wines are still usually sold with the brand or producer far more prominent than the region.

15

Vineyard in the Alentejo region showing above-ground tubing for irrigation.

MAIN PREMIUM QUALITY REGIONS

Traditionally, the best Portuguese red wines were high in tannins and acidity and were made from local varieties grown in the **Douro, Dão** and **Bairrada** DOCs in northern Portugal. Softer, fruitier wines are now being made in these regions, but many require a long period of bottle age before they mellow and show their best. Some of Portugal's best exports now come from the southeast (**Alentejo DOC** and **Vinho Regional Alentejano**). This hot region mainly produces full-bodied red wines made from local and international grape varieties. Dark fruit and spice aromas (blackberry, plum, liquorice) are often enhanced by oak, which adds toast and chocolate notes to these wines.

BULK/INEXPENSIVE PRODUCTION REGIONS

The most important of these is **Vinho Verde DOC**. These are unoaked, light-bodied wines with light alcohol, high acidity and a slight fizz. They have citrus and green fruit notes (lemon, apple) and can be quite vegetal (grass, green leaves). Those produced for the local market are generally dry, whereas most exported wines have medium sweetness.

Branded rosé wines are also successful, being exported in large volumes. In terms of style, they follow the Vinhos Verdes, with medium sweetness, high acidity and a slight sparkle, though the flavours will be more red fruit (redcurrant, raspberry).

16 | South Africa

The WO (Wine of Origin) scheme in South Africa controls regional labelling, as well as varietal and vintage details on bottles. Estates are also included in the WO scheme. An estate wine may not use any grapes that have been bought in rather than being grown by a named estate.

Vineyards in Stellenbosch, showing reservoirs that supply water for irrigating the vines.

South Africa's vineyards are clustered around the Cape of Good Hope, where breezes coming off the cold Atlantic Ocean help to cool an otherwise hot region. Districts near the coast benefit most from the cooling ocean breezes, and have the greatest potential for premium quality wines.

The most important WOs for premium wine production are:

Cabernet Sauvignon and **Merlot** (including blends)
Coastal
Stellenbosch

Chardonnay
Coastal

Sauvignon Blanc
Coastal
Constantia

Chenin Blanc is widely grown, mainly for large-volume inexpensive white wines. Most of these are medium-bodied, dry or off-dry, with citrus and tropical fruit flavours. Despite the hot climate conditions, the wines have medium or even high acidity. There are premium quality Chenin Blancs, some of which have oak flavours. Chenin Blanc is also used in blends, including Chenin-Blanc/Chardonnay, where its role is similar to that of Semillon in Australian Semillon/Chardonnay blends: it makes possible the production of large volumes at lower prices, and contributes some refreshing acidity and citrus fruit to the blend.

Pinotage is a black grape variety that was developed specially for the hot South African conditions. Varietal Pinotage comes in a range of styles, but is typically full-bodied, with medium tannins and red fruit flavours, often accompanied by vegetal and animal notes (tar, leather).

Australia

The most important grape varieties grown in Australia are Shiraz, Chardonnay, Cabernet Sauvignon, Semillon and Riesling. The Label Integrity Scheme controls regional, varietal and vintage labelling. Although there are some prestigious exceptions, the majority of wines with state or multi-state regional designations are large-volume, inexpensive wines.

17

Vineyards are spread widely across Australia. However, with the exception of the Hunter Valley, the most famous regions are found either along the southern coast, where they benefit from the effects of the cold southern oceans or, increasingly, in mountainous areas where altitude leads to lower temperatures.

The most important areas for premium wine production are:

Shiraz
Barossa Valley
Hunter Valley
McLaren Vale
Western Victoria
Western Australia
(This variety is grown throughout almost all the Australian winemaking regions.)

Chardonnay
Adelaide Hills
Hunter Valley
(Like Shiraz, this is very widely grown.)

Cabernet Sauvignon
Margaret River
Coonawarra

Semillon
Hunter Valley

Riesling
Clare Valley
Eden Valley

Inexpensive, high-volume wines rely primarily on the fruit grown in the hot inland areas, with irrigation waters supplied by the Murray, Darling and Murrumbidgee rivers. These are generally sold as 'South Eastern Australia', a regional designation that allows blending across most of Australia's wine producing regions. The higher-priced South Eastern Australia wines generally contain a higher proportion of fruit from the premium regions such as those listed above.

140-year old Shiraz vine in the Hill of Grace vineyard of Henschke, Gnadenberg, near Keyneton, South Australia (Eden Valley). Old vines such as these give small yields of grapes with intensely concentrated flavours. No vines of a similar age remain in France because the Phylloxera louse destroyed them in the nineteenth century.

A classic Australian blend of varieties. Shiraz supplies richness and soft spicy fruit; Cabernet Sauvignon supplies tannins and black fruit.

This is a multi-state region, often used for large volume inexpensive wines.

Hunter Valley Semillon is dry, light in body and alcohol, but high in acidity. It has delicate citrus aromas in youth, verging on neutrality. With age, it builds layers of complex toast, honey and nut flavours. Semillon wines from other parts of Australia can range from medium-bodied simple citrus wines, to intensely vegetal and pungent.

18 New Zealand

Most of New Zealand is either too mountainous or too wet to grow grapes, but there are ten main winegrowing regions. Most of these lie on the sunny east coast, but are spread over both North and South Islands. Within the regions there are some specific district names that can appear on wine labels. These include Wairau Valley (Marlborough), Gimblett Gravels (Hawkes Bay), and Martinborough (Wellington).

Pinot Noir vines covered in netting to protect the ripening crop from being eaten by birds.

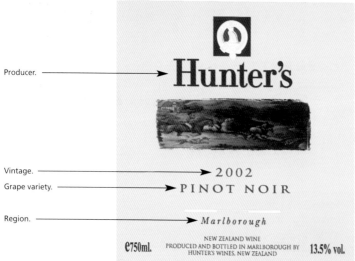

Producer.

Vintage.
Grape variety.

Region.

Hunter's

2002
PINOT NOIR

Marlborough

NEW ZEALAND WINE
℮750ml.   PRODUCED AND BOTTLED IN MARLBOROUGH BY   13.5% vol.
HUNTER'S WINES, NEW ZEALAND

The most important locations for premium wine production are:

Sauvignon Blanc
Marlborough

Chardonnay
Gisborne
Hawkes Bay
Marlborough

Pinot Noir
Martinborough
Marlborough
Central Otago

Cabernet Sauvignon and **Merlot** (including blends)
Hawkes Bay

Premium wines are also made from Alsatian varieties (Riesling, Pinot Gris, and Gewurztraminer), particularly in the cooler parts of South Island.

The USA

In the USA regional terms can be as vague as a whole state or as precise as a single vineyard. One increasingly popular term used in California is 'Coastal'. This allows blending across almost all the Californian vineyards lying up to 100km inland of the Pacific.

19

The varying effects of cool ocean breezes from the cold Pacific, mists that shield grapes from the morning sun, and – for vineyards located in the hills – altitude, mean that a wide range of climates, from cool to hot, can be found in California. Premium quality sites are also found further north in Oregon and Washington. The bulk of inexpensive production occurs in the hot, irrigated Central Valley in California, where the cooling ocean influence is minimal, but warmth and sunshine make it easy to obtain large crops of healthy, ripe grapes.

The most important locations for premium wine production are:

Cabernet Sauvignon and **Merlot** (including blends)
Napa Valley
Sonoma County

Chardonnay
Carneros
Napa Valley
Washington State

Sauvignon Blanc
Napa Valley

Pinot Noir
Carneros
Sonoma County
Oregon State

Zinfandel is a very important black grape variety for premium quality wines in California. Although much is used for off-dry fruity rosés, it shows its best in dry red wines. These are full-bodied, and high in alcohol, with flavours of black fruit, dried fruit and sweet spices (blackberry, prune, raisin, clove, liquorice). The most intense, complex wines are made from old vines: some Zinfandel vineyards were planted over 100 years ago.

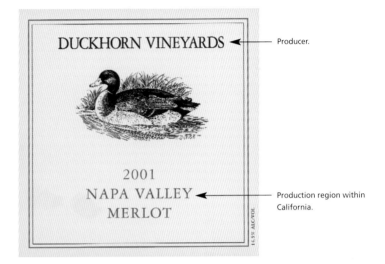

Producer.

Production region within California.

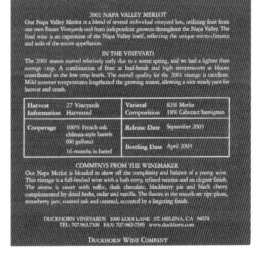

A very detailed back label. Note that this 'Merlot' contains 18% Cabernet Sauvignon. For many wines where regions, vintages and grape varieties are stated, a small percentage (usually up to 15%, more in California) of other varieties, vintages and regions may be used in the blend.

20   **Chile**   Chile has a system of regional DOs (denominations of origin) in which regions are divided into subregions. The names of these are usually taken from the rivers that flow from the Andes to the Pacific.

Sunshine, fertile soils, a mild moderate climate and meltwater from the Andes combine to create ideal conditions for the production of premium quality Cabernet Sauvignon and Merlot in the Colchagua Subregion of the Rapel Valley.

Most Chilean regions have fertile soils and a plentiful supply of irrigation water from rivers. The climate is generally hot, and most vines, especially for inexpensive wines, are planted on the floor of the Central Valley that runs north–south between the Coastal mountain range and the Andes. The best sites take advantage of cooling breezes and coastal fogs from the cold Pacific Ocean or, increasingly, altitude as vineyards are planted on hillside sites.

The most important locations for premium wines are:

    Cabernet Sauvignon and **Merlot** (including blends)
    Central Valley
    Rapel Valley
    Maipo Valley

Chardonnay
Central Valley
Casablanca Valley

Sauvignon Blanc
Casablanca Valley

Carmenère is also a very important black grape variety in Chile. It is originally a Bordeaux variety, which was introduced to Chile at the same time as Cabernet Sauvignon and Merlot. It is often used as a blend with these varieties. Varietal Carmenère wines are deep in colour, medium or full-bodied, with medium or high acidity and alcohol, and high levels of tannin. They have flavours of dark fruit (blackberry) and peppery spice. When underripe, Carmenère can show pungent green bell pepper and green bean flavours.

Argentina

Although Argentina had a system of DOCs (Controlled Denominations of Origin) before Chile, it is still much more common for the wines to be labelled by region (e.g. Mendoza, Río Negro, Cafayate).

21

The climate in the main Argentinian winegrowing regions is hot, sunny and very dry. The best sites take advantage of altitude to benefit from the cooler temperatures.

Malbec is the most important grape variety for premium red wines. This is originally a Bordeaux variety. It gives full-bodied wines with medium or high levels of tannin, which can make some Argentinean Malbecs suitable for ageing. The wines have a dark fruit character, often with spicy flavours (blackberry, black plum, clove, pepper), and the best wines benefit from oak ageing. It is common to blend Malbec with Cabernet Sauvignon and/or Merlot. It is grown widely in Argentina, but most plantings are in Mendoza.

Torrontés is a local speciality for white wines. It is an aromatic variety, giving medium-bodied dry white wines with high alcohol, medium acidity, and pronounced fruity/floral aromas (perfume, grapes, peach). Like Malbec, it is widely grown, but most of the best examples come from the Cafayate region.

The most important locations for other premium wines are:

Chardonnay
Mendoza

Cabernet Sauvignon and **Merlot**
Mendoza
Cafayate

In Mendoza rainfall is very low. Here, Malbec vines are being supplied with water by flooding the vineyard.

22 **Sparkling Wines**

Broadly speaking, quality sparkling wines can be divided into two categories. Some are intended to taste like fizzy versions of a still wine, and express the flavours of the grapes. These wines are generally made using the tank method. Others, in addition to flavours of the base wine, add complexities arising from ageing and the breakdown products of the yeasts that add the bubbles. These are generally bottle-fermented. In both cases, the dissolved carbon dioxide that makes the wine fizzy is a by-product of alcoholic fermentation.

Both tank method and bottle-fermented sparkling wines start with a still base wine. This will usually be light in alcohol, because these processes add approximately 1–2% abv, as well as carbon dioxide (CO_2) gas dissolved under pressure.

THE TANK METHOD

In this method, part of the fermentation takes place in a sealed tank, which prevents any carbon dioxide gas from escaping. This carbon dioxide dissolves in the wine, and in order to retain it, the wine must be bottled under pressure. When the bottle is opened, the dissolved carbon dioxide causes the wine to bubble.

The base wine could be partially fermented must, where the last part of the fermentation takes place in the sealed tank. Because the fermentation can be interrupted (by filtering out the yeast), this method is suitable for making sweet sparkling wines with light alcohol levels, such as Asti.

Alternatively the starting point could be a fully fermented dry wine, to which sugar and yeast are added and the fermentation restarted in the pressurised tank.

These two variations on the tank method are ideal for fresh, fruity styles of sparkling wine such as Asti, most Prosecco, and much Sekt.

Prosecco is a sparkling wine from northeast Italy. It is usually made using the tank method, though bottle-fermented versions (see below) also exist. The Prosecco grape variety gives a medium-bodied, dry or off-dry sparkling wine with delicate stone fruit flavours. Some are fully sparkling (*spumante*); others are just lightly sparkling (*frizzante*).

Asti DOCG is a sweet, fruity, light-bodied sparkling white from Piemonte in northwest Italy. It is made with the Muscat grape, which gives intense floral and fruity flavours (peach, grape, rose). It is usually fully sparkling, but wines labelled Moscato d'Asti just have a light sparkle.

Region. Champagne is an *Appellation Contrôlée* delimited region in northern France, but rarely uses the words *Appellation Contrôlée* on the label.

Producer. Epernay is one of the three major towns in the Champagne region, along with Ay and Reims.

Brut = bone dry. Most Champagnes are made in this style.

The small print tells you that this Champagne was made for Thierry Lesne by the Centre Vinicole in Chouilly.

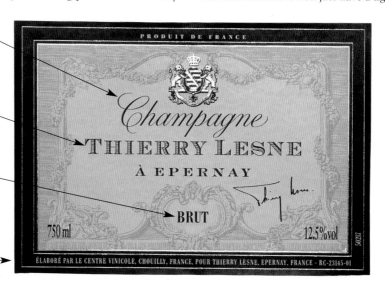

PRODUIT DE FRANCE

Champagne

THIERRY LESNE

À EPERNAY

BRUT

750 ml   12.5%vol

ÉLABORÉ PAR LE CENTRE VINICOLE, CHOUILLY, FRANCE, POUR THIERRY LESNE, EPERNAY, FRANCE - RC-23145-01

Sekt is simply the German word for sparkling wine. There are some very high quality, bottle-fermented Sekts made in both Germany and Austria. However, most are simple, inexpensive wines made from aromatic varieties using the tank method. These can be medium or dry, are generally light in body, with floral and fruity flavours. A wine labelled simply as **Sekt** will generally use cheap base wines sourced from anywhere within the EU. **Deutscher Sekt** can only be made from German base wines

BOTTLE-FERMENTED SPARKLING WINES

These methods are much more labour intensive than the tank method, and production costs are much higher. However, they have two main advantages in terms of quality. Firstly, through the extended contact the wine has with the dead yeast, the wines can gain complex bready, biscuity flavours that do not appear in other wines. Secondly, the bubbles in wines produced this way are much smaller, less aggressive and longer-lasting than the bubbles in tank-fermented sparkling wines.

First, a still, dry **base wine** is blended. A mixture of sugar and yeast is added, then the wine is bottled, sealed and stored. A **second fermentation** takes place, in which the wine increases slightly in alcohol, and the carbon dioxide, which cannot escape from the sealed bottle, becomes dissolved in the wine.

This slow fermentation is then followed by a period of ageing, during which a process called **yeast autolysis** ('self-digestion') occurs. The yeasts slowly release flavours into the wine. This is the most important part of the bottle fermentation process, and accounts for many of the special flavours that appear in these wines (these flavours are described as *autolytic*). This process could last for a number of months, or even several years.

After ageing, the next stage is to **disgorge** (remove) the yeasty deposit, otherwise it makes the wine hazy.

In the **traditional method**, the bottle is slowly tipped and jiggled so that the yeast cells slide into the neck of the bottle. This tipping and jiggling can be done by hand – by *'remueurs'* – but is usually done mechanically, by machines (gyropalettes) that can process hundreds of bottles at a time. The plug of yeast in the neck is then frozen, and pops out when the bottle is unsealed. The bottle is topped up with a mixture of wine and (usually) sugar. The amount of sugar added (the **dosage**) determines the sweetness of

Roman chalk quarries in Champagne now provide a cool, constant temperature – ideal conditions for extended ageing during the process of yeast autolysis. Although most champagne houses use gyropalettes to help remove the yeast deposit at the end of this process, here a *remueur* is doing the laborious job by hand.

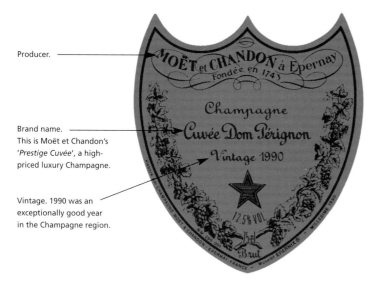

Producer.

Brand name.
This is Moët et Chandon's
'Prestige Cuvée', a high-
priced luxury Champagne.

Vintage. 1990 was an
exceptionally good year
in the Champagne region.

It has the major advantage of being less labour-intensive, with little impact on quality.

Champagne is the most famous bottle-fermented sparkling wine and is named after an AC region in northern France. The cool climate and chalky soils provide ideal conditions for base wines from Pinot Noir, Meunier and Chardonnay that are high in acidity but with medium body and light alcohol. Because the region is so cool, and weather varies from vintage to vintage, the grapes do not ripen fully every year. To achieve quality and consistency, most wines are **Non-Vintage**, and the base wine is a blend of several vintages. In exceptional years, a portion of the best wine may be used to make a **Vintage** Champagne. Because of high demand and limited supply, Champagne is never cheap. The least expensive Champagnes will generally see the minimum legal period of yeast autolysis (15 months), and can be made from the least-ripe grapes. They can be quite simple, with high acidity and green fruit flavours (green apple). Brands are very important in Champagne, ranging from BOBs (buyer's own brands) such as supermarket own labels, through cooperative-owned brands to the famous houses, known as *Grand Marques*. Many of the best producers give their wines a long period of ageing before release. The better wines are typically dry, with high acidity, and complex flavours of green and citrus fruit (apple, lemon), and autolytic notes (biscuit, bread, toast). Vintage

the final bottled product. Most wines made this way are 'Brut', which means that a very small amount of sugar is used, but because of the high acidity of most sparkling wines, the wine tastes dry. *Demi-sec* or *semi-seco* indicates medium sweetness.

An alternative method of removing the yeast is to empty the entire contents of the bottles into a tank under pressure. It is then filtered to remove the yeast, dosaged and rebottled. This **transfer method** is not permitted for Champagne or Cava, but it is common in New Zealand and Australia.

Gyropalettes in Seppelt's sparkling wine cellars, Great Western, Victoria, Australia. These rotate and move the bottles, causing the dead yeast deposit to slide into the neck of the bottle. Large gyropalettes can process over 2 000 bottles at a time.

Champagnes are particularly complex wines, combining intense fruity and autolytic flavours with vegetal complexity from bottle age.

Bottle-fermented sparkling wines are made in many other French regions. **Crémant** indicates a sparkling wine made using the traditional method. The major region for production is the Loire, particularly around **Saumur**, where Chenin Blanc is the main grape variety. These wines generally have high acidity and green and citrus fruit flavours, sometimes with some autolytic character, but they are rarely as complex as most Champagnes.

Cava is the Spanish term for traditional-method sparkling wines. The main grape varieties are local Spanish ones. The wines have fairly neutral fruit flavours (perhaps a hint of apple), medium acidity (less than Champagne), and very little autolytic complexity. Some houses use a portion of Chardonnay in the blend, which can give more complex wines. Most Cava is best consumed on release.

New Zealand, Australia, South Africa and **California** are important producers of bottle-fermented sparkling wines. Brands are extremely important here, as in Cava and Champagne, and the variety of styles makes it impossible to generalise. The best wines use the Champagne grape varieties (Pinot Noir, Meunier and Chardonnay), and can be very intense and complex with long length.

Sparkling Reds are a particular speciality in Australia. These are usually made with Shiraz. They are full-bodied, with medium acidity and intense black and red berry fruit notes. Some are fruity and off-dry; others are dry, with leathery complexity from aged reserve wines.

23 Sweet Wines

Yeast converts sugar to alcohol, and for almost all wines, red or white, the fermentation continues until no detectable sugar remains. The resulting wines are dry. For sweet wines, either the fermentation must be interrupted, or a sweet component added to sweeten the wine or, for some exceptional wines, the sugar levels in the grape juice are so high that sugar remains in the wine after the yeasts are killed by alcohol.

INTERRUPTING THE FERMENTATION

If the yeasts are stopped before they have finished converting all the sugar to alcohol, a sweet wine will result. This could be achieved by removing the yeasts using a fine filter to ensure none remain in the liquid. Or the yeast could be poisoned, using sulphur dioxide or alcohol. One common way to do this is to **fortify** (add alcohol) part way through the fermentation. This technique is used for Port as well as many fortified Muscat wines.

Sweet fortified Muscat wines are made widely around the Mediterranean from Greece to Portugal. They include *Vins Doux Naturels* such as **Muscat de Beaumes de Venise**, and **Muscat de Rivesaltes** from southern France. These are generally released, unaged, and are best consumed soon after production while the intensely fruity aromas (grape, peach, perfume) are at their freshest. The wines are medium or full-bodied, and sweet, with high alcohol and medium or low acidity. **Moscatel de Valencia** is an inexpensive sweet fortified Muscat wine from Spain.

Sweet fortified Muscat wines are also made in other parts of the world, and are a particular speciality in Australia. **Rutherglen Muscats**, from a hot region in northern Victoria, are aged for a long period in oak. This causes the wine to oxidise and develop complex dried-fruit and kernel flavours (raisin, prune, fig, dried apricot, coffee, toffee). They are sweet and full-bodied, with high alcohol and medium or low acidity.

ADDING A SWEET COMPONENT TO THE BLEND

Adding sugar to wines to make them sweet is not permitted. However, some sweet liquids can be used for sweetening. These include the unfermented grape juice (*süssreserve*) used to sweeten many medium or sweet German wines. Apart from Pedro Ximénez, the traditional styles of Sherry (Fino, Amontillado and Oloroso) are dry. Sweet Pedro Ximénez Sherry, or mixes of grape juice and alcohol, or concentrated grape juice may be added to make medium and sweet Sherries such as Oloroso Dulce, commercial Amontillados, and Pale Creams.

CONCENTRATION OF SUGARS IN THE GRAPES

This group of methods is used for most of the greatest sweet wines. Yeasts die when the alcohol level reaches around 15% abv. If there is still some

Château name. This château was overlooked in the 1855 classification although it is surrounded by *Premier Cru Classé* châteaux and produces wine of *Premier Cru Classé* quality.

Region and EU quality category (QWPSR).

Vintage. Extremely important in regions like Sauternes which rely on a particular combination of weather conditions to make their wine.

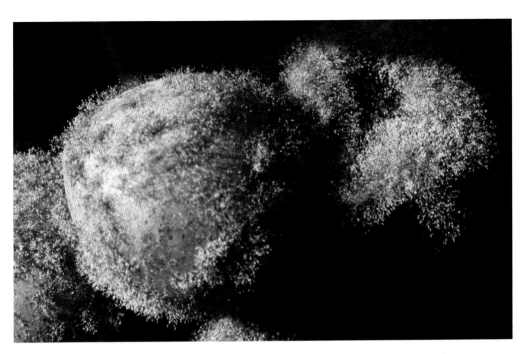

Botrytis (noble rot)
growing on Sémillon
grapes in Sauternes.

sugar left, then this will remain in the finished wine. The required sugar levels to achieve above 15% abv are not found in normally ripened grapes. However, there are ways of concentrating the sugar levels in the grape. One method is to **dry the grapes**. A variation on this method is to take advantage of **noble rot**. A third method is to **freeze the grapes**.

Dried Grape Wines

Drying the grapes causes them to shrivel. This could occur on the vine, with some late-harvested grapes, or it can be done by laying the grapes out in well-ventilated, dry conditions that encourage evaporation. Sweet wines made this way include Recioto wines from Italy. An extreme example is PX (Pedro Ximénez) Sherry (see Chapter 24).

Noble Rot Wines

Noble rot, or *Botrytis cinerea*, is an important part of the production of many classic sweet wines, including Sauternes, Tokaji, Austrian and German BA (*Beerenauslese*) and TBA (*Trockenbeerenauslese*) wines, and the sweet wines of the Loire. When *Botrytis cinerea* mould attacks healthy, ripe grapes, it weakens the skin, speeding up the evaporation of water from the flesh of the grapes and causing them to shrivel. As well as concentrating sugars and acids, the mould adds its own unique flavours to the wine. A combination of factors is needed to make these wines: a problem-free ripening period to ensure fully ripe, healthy grapes; damp, misty mornings to encourage the growth and spread of the botrytis mould; and warm dry afternoons to speed the drying out of the grapes. Such conditions are found in very few wine growing regions, and cannot be relied on to occur every year.

The mould rarely affects all of the grapes evenly, which means that several passes may have to be made through the vineyard to pick all the grapes at the perfect stage of rottenness. Hand-picking is essential, and the laborious process of grape selection makes these wines expensive to produce. Where these wines sell at more modest prices, it is often because a less rigorous selection of grapes is used.

Certain grape varieties are particularly susceptible to noble rot, including Riesling, Sémillon and Chenin Blanc. The characteristic

Producer.

Vintage.

Region and style. Aszú wines are the famous sweet wines of Tokaji, though medium and dry wines are also made.

5 *puttonyos* indicates the level of sweetness (6 is the maximum, 5 is extremely sweet).

Tokaji is usually bottled in dumpy 500ml bottles, rather than the usual 750ml.

This is a single vineyard within the Tokaji region, rated second class in 1700, a very high rating.

Riesling grapes protected from the rain and birds by plastic sheeting, in the hope of making *Eiswein*. Rauenthal, Germany (Rheingau).

aromas of noble rot are hard to describe, and the best way to recognise them is to try a few examples of these wines. Words that have been used include dried apricot, ryebread, sweet biscuits, cabbage, orange marmalade, pineapple and mushroom.

Sauternes AC is a region to the south of Graves AC in Bordeaux. Sémillon is the main grape variety, though Sauvignon Blanc is also used to add acidity and aromatic fruit flavours. Luscious sweetness is balanced by high acidity. These full-bodied wines have high alcohol and citrus stone fruit and botrytis flavours (lemon, peach), and often a hint of new oak (vanilla, toast, coffee). These wines age well, gaining vegetal complexity in the bottle.

Tokaji is a wine from northeastern Hungary. Although some dry and medium wines are made, the most famous wines are the sweet Tokaji Aszú. These are classified with a number of *puttonyos*, indicating the level of sweetness in the wine. The sweetest is 6 *puttonyos*, but even a 3 *puttonyos* wine is sweet. Tokaji wines are amber in colour, due to a long period of ageing in oak. They are full-bodied, sweet, with medium alcohol and high acidity. They have intense flavours of dried fruits and sweet spices (orange peel, orange marmalade, dried apricots, raisins, cinnamon, ryebread). These wines age well, gaining notes of nut, coffee, caramel and honey.

Sweet and rare **BA** (**Beerenauslese**) wines and the even sweeter and rarer **TBA** (**Trockenbeerenauslese**) wines are Prädikatswein quality categories in Germany and Austria (see Chapter 12). In order

This indicates that a combination of drying and botrytis has been used to concentrate sugars and flavours in this wine. Shortly before the harvest the canes have been cut, interrupting the water supply from the roots to the fruit. This speeds up the process of evaporation which botrytis also accelerates.

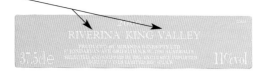

PRODUCE OF AUSTRALIA

Late Cut

BOTRYTIS

RIVERINA KING VALLEY

37.5cl

Grapes from two regions are used. Reservoirs for irrigation in Riverina (a bulk production region in New South Wales) encourage late season botrytis.

to be classified as a BA or a TBA, the levels of sugar in the must are so high that they can normally only be achieved with the help of botrytis. These wines have low alcohol, light or medium body, and are very sweet with high acidity. Flavours depend on the grape variety used, but generally intense botrytis flavours are accompanied by dried fruit notes (dried apricot, raisin). In Germany, the finest BAs and TBAs are made with Riesling, generally from steep vineyard sites above the Rhine and Mosel.

Botrytis-affected sweet wines are also made in **Coteaux du Layon AC, Vouvray AC,** and other Loire appellations, from Chenin Blanc. In **Alsace AC,** botrytis-affected sweet wines are occasionally made from Riesling, Gewurztraminer, Pinot Gris or Muscat.

Australia produces good quantities of botrytis-affected sweet wines, mainly using Semillon or Riesling.

Frozen Grape Wines

In Canada, Germany and Austria, healthy grapes are sometimes left on the vine and harvested in winter while the water in them is frozen. The grapes are crushed while still frozen so that the ice crystals can be removed, leaving an intensely concentrated sugary grape syrup that is used to make sweet **Eiswein** or **icewine.** Because these are made with intensely concentrated juice from

Producer.

Grape variety.
Vidal is a hardy variety, and is well suited to harsh Canadian winters.

Icewine.

VQA is Canada's body that regulates the statements of vintage, grape variety, or regions on wine labels, and controls winemaking standards.

healthy grapes, the wines have very pure, pronounced, varietal-fruity flavours, high acidity, full body and syrupy sweetness. Riesling is the main grape used in Germany.

24 Sherry and Port

Sherry is a dry, medium or sweet fortified wine made around the town of Jerez de la Frontera in southern Spain. The base wine for all Sherries is a neutral white wine, though after its special ageing process the final product can be amber or even deep brown in colour. Port is a sweet fortified wine made from grapes grown in the upper Douro in Portugal. Although white Port exists, most Port is purple, ruby or tawny in colour, depending on how it has been aged.

SHERRY PRODUCTION

There are many different styles of Sherry, but the starting point for almost all is a neutral, dry, low-acid wine made from the Palomino grape variety. Alcohol is added to fortify the wine, before it goes through the *solera* ageing process.

Sherry is matured in old casks that contain the wine but do not give it any oak flavours. Maturation takes place using the solera system. This is a technique which blends younger and older wines together continually as they age. It ensures a consistent style of mature wine. Most of the flavours in a Sherry come from this ageing process, and the differences in style between Sherries are due to differences in their ageing periods and conditions.

SHERRY STYLES

Fino and **Manzanilla** Sherries are pale in colour, dry, medium-bodied, typically with around 15% abv. The wine is kept fresh during the *solera* ageing process by a layer of yeast known as 'flor', which floats on the wine. This layer of flor protects the wine from air that would otherwise spoil it. The yeast gives unusual bready notes to the wine, which has refreshing citrus zest and almond flavours. After bottling, these wines rapidly lose their freshness, so they should be consumed, chilled, as quickly as possible. **Pale Cream** Sherries are young Finos that have been sweetened with concentrated grape juice.

Amontillado Sherries are made by taking a Fino or Manzanilla, and adding more spirit to increase the alcohol and so kill off the flor.

These are three particularly good examples of the traditional dry styles of Sherry.

Fino.

Amontillado.

Oloroso.

With no protection, the wine begins to oxidise. Amontillados have a deeper, amber colour and nutty flavours. When they are removed from the *solera*, Amontillados are dry wines. However, for some markets, it is common for them to be sweetened before bottling, with the result that many commercial Amontillados have medium sweetness.

Oloroso Sherries are fortified after fermentation to 18% abv. At that strength, flor will not grow so oxygen attacks them throughout their ageing. Oloroso wines are deep brown, and full-bodied with high alcohol. The oxidation results in intense kernel and animal flavours (roasted nuts, coffee, meat). As with Amontillado Sherries, these are dry when they are drawn from the *solera*, but it is even more common for sweetening to occur before bottling. These may be labelled as **Oloroso Dulce**, or **Cream** Sherries.

PX (Pedro Ximénez) are intensely sweet Sherries made from sun-dried Pedro Ximénez grapes. The wines are almost black, with intense dried fruit flavours (fig, prune, raisin, sultana). They are full-bodied, and syrupy in texture due to their extremely high sugar content. These are used as the sweetening component of the finest sweetened Sherries.

PORT PRODUCTION

Port is made from a blend of black grape varieties. Sufficient colour and tannins are vigorously extracted from the skins. Then, while there is still a high proportion of sugar in the must, grape-derived spirit is mixed with the partly fermented grape juice. This kills off the yeasts, stopping the fermentation, and results in a wine that is sugary and high in alcohol. The wine is then aged in large oak vessels for a period before vatting and bottling.

PORT STYLES
Ruby Style Port

Inexpensive **Ruby Port** is a non-vintage wine that generally undergoes less than three years' ageing before bottling. These are simple, fruity wines.

Reserve Ruby Port uses better quality wines, with more intense, complex fruit flavours. Longer cask ageing (up to five years) helps to soften and integrate the alcohol.

Late Bottled Vintage (LBV) Port is similar in style to a Reserve Ruby, but the wines come from a single year's harvest. Most do not need to be decanted, but those labelled **Traditional Style LBV** have not been filtered before bottling, and will have a deposit that requires decanting. All of these wines are ready to drink on release. Most show

intense red and black fruit flavours (cherry, plum, blackberry), often with a hint of sweet spice (clove, pepper). They are sweet, with high alcohol, little or no tannins and medium or low acidity.

Vintage Ports

Vintage Ports (including **Single Quinta Vintage Ports**) are very long-lived wines. The grapes come from the very best vineyards, and these wines are only made in good years. They are bottled,

Sherries are aged for long periods in a *solera* such as this. The ageing process accounts for most of the flavour of Sherry: the base wine from which it is made is fairly neutral in character.

Steep terraced vineyards on barren soils in the Douro Region in northern Portugal, source of the grapes for Port production.

unfiltered, after a short period in oak. Unlike Ruby and LBV Ports, these initially have high levels of tannin, as well as intense fruit flavours, sweetness and high alcohol. Although they can be enjoyed while still youthful, Vintage Ports benefit greatly from bottle age. The intense, spicy red and black fruit aromas of youth evolve into cooked fruit, animal and vegetal notes (prune, leather, wet leaves, coffee). As they age, these ports leave a large deposit, so they *must* be decanted.

Both of these bottles use the word 'vintage' on the label, but only the Quinta do Vesuvio is a 'true' Vintage Port. LBV ports are usually stripped of the tannins that would enable them to benefit from cellaring. They are ready to drink on release and do not need decanting.

Tawny Ports

Inexpensive **Tawny Port** is a lighter style of Port, pink rather than deep red in colour, with toffee and caramel flavours. They are usually made by mixing paler-coloured ruby ports with some inexpensive white Port (Port made from white grape varieties). By contrast, **Reserve Tawny Ports** are made by ageing the wine for at least seven years in oak. This breaks down the intense fruit flavours, and encourages oxidative, kernel flavours to develop (walnut, coffee, chocolate, caramel). Oxygen also attacks the colour, and these wines are a medium tawny in appearance, rather than the opaque purple, ruby or garnet of other Ports. The very best of these are the **Tawny Ports with Indication of Age,** which could be labelled as 10, 20, 30 or **over 40 years old.** The stated age is an average, not a minimum. These ports do not need to be decanted, because they do not form a deposit. They are best consumed as close to the bottling date as possible (this date is usually on the front or back label). Whereas other styles of Port should be served at room temperature, Tawny Ports are best served slightly chilled.

25 The Distillation Process

Distillation is a process that takes one component of a liquid, and concentrates it. For the production of spirits, the aim is to increase the alcohol content of the liquid.

When increasing the alcohol content of a liquid, advantage can be taken of the fact that ethanol (drinkable alcohol) boils at a lower temperature than water. By warming an alcoholic liquid, the alcohol can be boiled off, and then collected, cooled and condensed back into a higher-strength alcoholic liquid. The water, which constitutes the largest proportion of fermented alcoholic drinks, is mostly left behind, along with any solids, colour compounds and unfermented sugars. This process is carried out in a still. There are many different kinds of still, but they can be divided into two broad categories.

POT STILLS

The **pot still** is the oldest, simplest kind of still. The pot is a vessel, usually made of copper, that contains the base alcoholic liquid while it is being heated. A neck extends above the pot like a chimney; the alcohol vapours collect in this as they are boiled off. Vapours in the neck then flow into a condenser, which uses cold water to condense them back into a stronger alcoholic liquid.

The most volatile components, which boil off first, are called the **heads** (or foreshots). They contain concentrated poisons, including methanol. The **hearts** (or spirit) follow. This part contains the highest proportion of ethanol, and the lowest proportion of undesirable impurities. The least volatile components, known as the **tails** (or feints), boil off last. Heads and tails are not used in the final spirit; they are returned to the pot to be redistilled with the next batch because they include some desirable ethanol.

Pot distillation is a cumbersome batch process. Because it is relatively inefficient, two or more successive distillations are needed to obtain a spirit of sufficient strength. Even with multiple distillations, the spirits produced are far from pure.

CONTINUOUS (COLUMN) STILLS

The **continuous still** is a nineteenth-century invention. It addresses the weaknesses of the pot still. In a single distillation it can produce a liquid that is very close to pure ethanol. It is not a batch process, so it can be run continuously and efficiently. The design is quite complex, and there are many variations. Some column stills are deliberately designed to produce a lower-strength spirit with more impurities and therefore more flavour.

SPIRIT STRENGTH AND CHARACTERISTICS

As a general rule, the purest, highest-strength spirits are the lightest in flavour and character. When reduced (watered down) to a standard bottling strength of around 40% abv, these spirits are relatively smooth, so they can be bottled and consumed without further maturation. Conversely, spirits that are lower-strength when they come off the still contain more impurities and more flavour character, including that of the base material (barley, maize, apples, grapes, cherries, sugarcane, agave and so on). However, these impurities also make the spirit harsher, so they generally need to be matured in oak or charcoal-filtered to soften them.

All spirits are water-white when they come off the still. Any colour in the final spirit comes

This diagram shows the inner workings of a Cognac Pot Still, similar to the one illustrated on page 72. Although pot stills used for other spirits vary in size, shape and material (most are made of copper), the processes of evaporation followed by condensation are common to all.

Cognac pot still

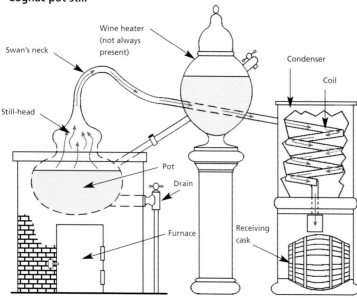

Swan's neck
Wine heater (not always present)
Still-head
Condenser
Coil
Pot
Drain
Furnace
Receiving cask

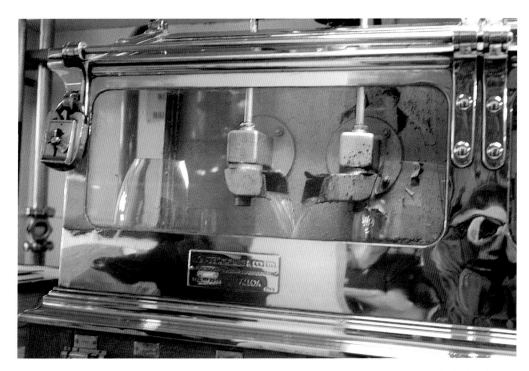

Whether a pot still (see diagram below) or column still is used, sugars and colours are left behind. New make spirit is always water-white and bone-dry. Here we see water-white new-make spirit coming off the stills at Lagavulin Malt Whisky Distillery in Islay.

either from colourings, such as caramel, or from the effects of oak ageing. Because sugar is non-volatile, all spirits are bone dry when they come off the still. Any sweetness in the final bottled product is either added (e.g. with dark rums), or comes from the breakdown of oak into sugars during ageing (e.g. in Bourbon). Alcohol itself also has a slightly sweet flavour. The tannins and most acids that appear in fermented alcoholic drinks are also non-volatile, so they do not appear in the spirit. However, tannins can be absorbed from oak barrels during maturation.

26 | Spirit Styles

Spirits are high-strength alcoholic liquids produced by distillation. Their flavour depends on the type of distillation process (high strength neutral or low strength characterful); the base alcoholic liquid used (the type of fruit, grain or vegetable); and on the maturation they receive after distillation (period in oak, type of oak).

A copper pot still in the Cognac region. The pot is hidden by the brick structure on the right hand side. The *Swan's neck* collects vapours which are condensed in the condenser on the left, before being collected in the barrel in front.

BRANDY AND OTHER FRUIT SPIRITS

Wine is made by fermenting whole, fresh grapes. If this is distilled, the product is brandy. Most brandy is aged in oak and/or coloured with caramel before bottling, so it is brown or amber in colour.

Cognac and Armagnac

Cognac is an oak-aged grape brandy from a delimited region to the north of Bordeaux. It must be made using a copper pot still, with the result that Cognacs generally have distinctly fruity-floral aromas (grapes, perfume). They are medium to light in body, with smooth alcohol.

Armagnac is an oak-aged grape brandy that comes from a delimited area to the south of Bordeaux. Copper pot stills are permitted, but most Armagnac is made using a version of the column still that gives a relatively low-strength spirit that is quite harsh but full of character. Armagnac typically shows dried-fruit aromas (prune, raisin, fig) and is medium or full-bodied, with sometimes quite harsh alcohol.

Both Cognac and Armagnac must be aged in oak for a period before bottling. This maturation makes the spirit smoother, and adds oaky flavours (vanilla, coconut, toast, nuts, sweet spices). The terms **VS**, **VSOP** and **XO** (Napoleon) indicate increasing age. The minimum ageing periods for these terms are set in law, though many companies age components of their blends for much longer than the legal minimum.

Other French Brandies

Much grape brandy is produced in France outside the delimited Cognac and Armagnac regions. These seldom have the character or complexity of Armagnac or Cognac. They are generally made using continuous stills. There are no legal limits on the use of terms such as VS and Napoleon, so they may be quite harsh due to their short maturation period. Much of the colour comes from adding caramel, and they are often sweetened with sugar.

Spanish Brandies

Spain is a major producer of Brandy. Spanish brandies are generally deep in colour, full-bodied, with medium sweetness (added sugar) and dried fruit and sweet spice flavours (prune, fig, cinnamon, clove). The Sherry region is a major production area (Brandy de Jerez).

Other Fruit Spirits

As well as using whole fresh grapes, spirits can be

Delimited production region.

Producer.

XO indicates a very long period of ageing before bottling.

Grande Champagne is a delimited subzone of the Cognac region (in this context it is nothing to do with the Champagne region). The finest, most ageworthy Cognacs come from this subzone.

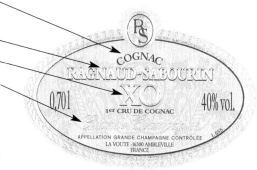

COGNAC
RAGNAUD-SABOURIN
0,70l   XO   40% vol.
1er CRU DE COGNAC
APPELLATION GRANDE CHAMPAGNE CONTRÔLÉE
LA VOUTE -16300 AMBLEVILLE
FRANCE

Copper pot stills are an inefficient method of concentrating alcohol in a liquid. Multiple distillations are usually needed to achieve a spirit of the desired strength. Here there are three stills working in succession to produce spirit for Auchentochan single malt.

made by distilling the grapeskins or residue left over from fermentation. These spirits are known as Marc or Grappa. Fruits other than grapes can be used too: Calvados is made with distilled, fermented apples or pears from a delimited region in northern France. Eaux-de-Vie (spirits) are made from many other fruits, including pears, cherries and plums.

WHISKIES

Whiskies are characterful oak-aged spirits made from grains such as barley, maize and rye. Unlike grapes, grains contain starch rather than sugar, and are solid rather than liquid. The **conversion** of starch into fermentable sugars takes place after the starch has been extracted from the coarsely-ground grains using hot water. This is the same process used in the production of beer. Whisky can be thought of as a distilled beer that is then matured in oak. The beer used is different from most beers we consume: it is not flavoured with hops, is high in strength, and in some cases may have strong peaty flavours.

Scotch Whisky

Scotch whisky must be distilled in Scotland, and aged in oak casks in Scotland for at least three years. An age statement on the bottle indicates the age of the youngest component.

Malt whisky is made using only malted barley. This is barley that has been allowed to start germinating to begin the conversion of starch into sugar; germination is then interrupted by drying

Unusually, this single malt whisky comes from an unblended, single cask. Because it is not a blend of several casks of different ages, it can state the year it was distilled. In this case: 1967.

Islay produces particularly pungent, peaty, medicinal single malt whiskies.

Most whiskies, even single malts, are blends of many barrels, often of differing ages. This whisky all came from a single cask. 32 years is a long time to spend ageing. Some old whiskies are very complex, (others are tired, stale and woody).

This is a higher than normal bottling strength, but whiskies that are not chill-filtered are liable to turn cloudy in cold conditions if they are bottled at 40% abv. Some believe chill filtration strips the whisky of character and prefer to bottle at a higher strength.

Name of the distillery.

the barley in a kiln; where peat is used as a fuel for the kilning process, this is the source of the smokey flavours characteristic of many Scotch whiskies. Distillation must take place in copper pot stills.

A **single malt whisky** is a malt whisky that comes from just one distillery. (Blends of malt whiskies from more than one distillery may be labelled as blended malts.) Single malt whiskies vary greatly in style depending on how they are made. The level of peat used when kilning the barley, the type of cask used for maturation, and the length of maturation can have as much impact on the flavour as the distillery location, shape of the stills, or the water source. Because of these variations, it is impossible to generalise about styles. Usually there will be some degree of peaty smokiness, and other flavours may include floral, honey, fruity, dried fruit, nutty, medicinal, spicy, cereal and woody notes.

More detail about the typical regional styles of Highland, Islay, Speyside and Lowland single malts is found in the Glossary.

Blended Scotch whisky is a blend of malt and grain whisky. A grain whisky is made in a column still, using a combination of malted barley and other grains (such as wheat or maize and unmalted barley). Compared to a single malt, the spirit component of a grain whisky is less harsh, but less flavoursome when it comes off the still, and there is less need to soften it through a long period in oak. The quality and character of a blended whisky will depend on the characteristics of its component parts (malts and grain), and how well they are matched together. Some blended whiskies are intense in flavour; others are more delicate. Some have almost no peaty/smoky flavours; others are noticeably peaty. The best blended whiskies have a smooth spirit component and a well-balanced combination of flavours.

Irish Whiskey

Irish whiskies are generally made from a mixture of malted and unmalted barley, and other grains, though there are some Irish malt whiskies. They are usually unpeated, though some use peat. They generally use a combination of pot still and column still components, though some pure pot still Irish whiskies are made. They tend to be smooth, soft and mellow, with fruity, honey, floral and woody flavours.

American Whiskies

Bourbon is made using a mixture of grains, though the majority must be maize. Usually these are made using a combination of a column still

Although most rums are made from molasses, some are made from sugarcane juice. All trace their origins to the sugarcane plant, being harvested here.

and a pot still. These are run to produce a relatively low-strength spirit with harsh alcohol and robust flavours. Much of the character comes from ageing the spirit in heavily charred new American oak barrels. In fierce hot summers and cold winters, the spirit rapidly extracts colour and flavours from the barrel. Cereal flavours from the base material combine with sweet coconut and vanilla flavours from the oak. Fruit, honey and floral components can also develop.

Tennessee whiskey is produced in a similar way, but is filtered through maple wood charcoal before bottling. This results in a smoother spirit, and adds sweet, smoky flavours.

Most **Canadian** whisky is large-volume, inexpensive production and contains a high proportion of neutral bulk spirit.

RUM

The base material for most rums is molasses, which is a by-product of the sugar industry. This is diluted with water so that it can be fermented and then distilled. A few rums are made with sugarcane juice. Though some rums are distilled in pot stills, the majority are made using column stills. It is common to divide rums into white, golden and dark rums. Note that white rums may have been aged in oak and then stripped of colour by charcoal filtration. Dark rums may have seen little or no oak ageing; the colour frequently comes from added caramel.

White Rum

By far the most common style of light/white rum is the Cuban style. This is distilled to a high strength, and is dry and neutral in character, rather like vodka. Some brands of white rum are distilled to a lower strength, and have very intense tropical fruit flavours. A few are made with sugarcane juice, rather than molasses. These can have refreshing grassy, green fruit aromas.

Golden Rum

Golden rums are usually dry or off-dry, with smooth spirit due to a period of oak ageing. The better ones have intense, complex, fruity and oak aromas (banana, coconut, toffee).

Dark Rum

Many dark rums are blends of rums from various origins, chosen for the character and balance they contribute to the final product. They are generally full-bodied and sweet in style, with dried fruit and sweet spice flavours (fig, raisin, clove, cinnamon). Those where most of the colour comes from added caramel may be harsh and spirity. The best

are aged for several years in oak, and can be very smooth, intense and complex spirits.

TEQUILA

Tequila is made from the Blue Agave. This is not a cactus, but a succulent that is related to the yucca. It has a starchy core that is cooked to convert the starch into sugars. These sugars are then extracted, fermented and distilled to make Tequila. Blue Agave for the production of Tequila must come from the delimited Tequila region in Mexico.

Tequila styles

For many purists, **plata** (silver or white) Tequilas are the most authentic expression of an agave-based spirit. They are dry, with intense vegetal and spicy flavours (green pepper, peppercorn). Many **golden** Tequilas are simply unaged Tequilas that are coloured with caramel. Look for the words **reposado** (rested for a short time), or **añejo** (aged), if you seek a spirit that has been softened by a period in oak. A long period in oak can add complex woody flavours to the spirit, but tends to mask the character of the agave.

VODKA

Any fermentable material can be used as a base for vodka, including grapes and potatoes, though the most common materials are grains, especially barley, wheat and rye. The most important factor is that the spirit is distilled to such a high strength that little of the character of the base material remains. This will usually be achieved using a column still, though some pot-still vodkas exist. Many vodkas are filtered through charcoal to remove flavour and impurities, and then reduced to a bottling strength of around 40% abv before bottling. They do not need to be aged.

Vodka Styles

Most vodkas are made to be as neutral as possible. These are ideal for cocktails where the flavours of the other components are supposed to shine. Other vodkas are more characterful. These include many Polish and Russian vodkas, and some premium western vodkas. The flavours of these are still delicate, compared to those of any whisky or brandy, but hints of the base material (grain, grape, potato) will show on the nose and the palate.

FLAVOURED SPIRITS

There are many spirits made by adding flavourings to a neutral base spirit. These include flavoured vodkas, and other categories such as Gin, Pastis and bitters.

The base for Gin is a neutral white spirit, usually produced in a continuous still. For the best Gins (distilled gins) the addition of botanical flavourings involves a further distillation in copper pot stills such as these, which helps 'fix' the flavours in the Gin.

Gin

Gin is a dry, white spirit flavoured with a range of botanicals, including coriander, angelica and citrus peel, but the dominant flavour always comes from juniper. The very cheapest gins simply add flavour essences to the neutral spirit (**cold compounding**). **Distilled Gin** or **London Dry Gin** on the label indicates that a superior method is used to fix the flavourings, such as soaking the botanicals in the spirit, followed by distillation in a pot still. The flavours of these distilled gins are more intense and persistent.

Other Flavoured Spirits

Pastis is a spirit that is flavoured with a combination of herbs and spices, with anise dominating. This family of spirits with sweet spicy flavours of liquorice and/or aniseed also includes Absinthe and Ouzo.

Bitters are spirits that have been flavoured with bitter herbs and spices, sometimes with other flavourings such as bitter orange peel.

Liqueurs

A liqueur is a sweetened liquid that contains a portion of distilled spirit. Most liqueurs are also flavoured and coloured. The spirit component could be a classic spirit such as rum or cognac, or it could be high-strength, neutral ethanol. The flavouring could come from fruits, herbs, kernels or nuts, or farmyard products such as milk or eggs.

27

Many inexpensive liqueurs use synthetic flavourings and colouring. This can make an enormous difference. For example, liqueurs made using real cherries or orange peel have a much more natural, genuine, persistent flavour than those using artificial flavours. This difference will be reflected in the price.

Note also the difference between a liqueur, such as cherry brandy, which is made by flavouring a sweetened spirit with cherries, and its distilled fruit spirit equivalent, made by the distillation of fermented cherry sugars. The spirit will be dry and higher in alcohol than the liqueur, but generally much more expensive.

Fruit
Blackcurrant: Crème de Cassis
Apricot: Apricot Brandy
Cherry: Cherry Brandy, Heering Cherry Liqueur, Maraschino
Orange: Curaçao, Cointreau, Grand Marnier
Peach: Southern Comfort

Herb
Multi-herb: Galliano, Bénédictine, Chartreuse, Drambuie
Seed: Kummel
Mint: Crème de Menthe

Bean, Kernel, Nut
Coffee: Kahlua, Tia Maria
Chocolate: Crème de Cacao
Nuts: Amaretto, Malibu

Dairy
Egg: Advocaat
Cream: Bailey's Irish Cream

Appendix 1: Storage and Service

STORAGE OF WINE

If a wine is incorrectly stored it can affect the flavour and in severe cases, the wine will become faulty.

The following general points should be followed when storing wine:

- For long-term storage, the temperature for all wines should be cool and constant, preferably between 10 and 15°C, as extremes of cold and heat can cause damage. One of the worst places for long-term storage is in a kitchen, due to the wide fluctuations in temperature. Extended periods of refrigeration can cause corks to harden and lose their elasticity, with the result that the seal fails and air can attack the wine causing it to become stale. Sparkling wines lose their fizz.
- Store wine on its side to ensure the cork remains in contact with the wine. If the cork dries out it can let in air, and the air will oxidise the wine.
- Keep wines away from strong light. Natural sunshine or artificial light will heat the wine and it will become stale and old before its time. Artificial light can cause unpleasant flavours to develop in some wines.
- Keep wine away from vibrations, in order for it to lie undisturbed.

SERVICE OF WINE
Service temperatures

STYLE OF WINE	EXAMPLE OF STYLE OF WINE	SERVICE TEMPERATURE
Medium/full-bodied, oaked white	White Burgundy, Fumé Blanc	Lightly chilled 12°C
Light/medium-bodied white	Muscadet, Pinot Grigio, New Zealand Sauvignon Blanc, Fino Sherry	Chilled 10°C
Sweet wines	Sauternes, Sweet Muscats	Well chilled 6–8°C
Sparkling wines	Champagne, Cava, Asti	Well chilled 6–8°C
Light-bodied red	Beaujolais, Bardolino, Valpolicella	Lightly chilled 12°C
Medium/full-bodied red	Claret, Red Burgundy, Rioja, Australian Shiraz, Châteauneuf-du-Pape, Barolo, Amarone della Valpolicella, Vintage Port	Room temperature 17–18°C

Note that over-chilling can mask the flavours in white wines.
Note that the average room temperature will vary with the time of year and/or heating or air conditioning. If reds are too cold, they will taste thin and harsh. The most gentle way to warm them is by holding the bowl of the glass in your hands. Do not warm reds on a radiator, as they will lose their fruitiness and taste murky, thick and muddy.

Ice buckets or wine coolers are often used to keep white, rosé and sparkling wines cold. An ice bucket should be filled three-quarters full with equal quantities of ice and water so that the bottle is fully surrounded by iced water. The water is then able to

transfer the heat from the bottle to melt the ice (air acts as an insulator and a bottle in ice alone will chill very slowly until some of the ice has melted).

Glassware

An enormous range of glass shapes and sizes is used for the service of wine, each designed to emphasise a particular wine's characteristics. The use of the correct glass will enhance the drinking experience.

- **Red wines** are best served in larger-sized glasses. This will allow air to come into contact with a large wine surface and develop the aromas and flavours.
- **White** and **rosé wines** require medium-sized glasses so that the fresh, fruit characteristics are gathered and directed towards the top of the glass.
- **Sparkling wines** are best served in flute glasses. This shape enhances the effect of the bubbles (and thus the wine's aroma), allowing them to travel through a larger volume of the wine before bursting at the top of the glass. For this reason the old-style, saucer-shaped glasses are completely inappropriate, as the bubbles are very quickly lost.
- **Fortified wines** should be served in small glasses to emphasise the fruit characteristics rather than the alcohol. However, the glass should be large enough to allow swirling and nosing.

Clean glassware is of the utmost importance, as even the slightest taint can ruin the flavour of the wine. This can also apply to 'clean' glasses from a dishwasher; it is worth checking the glasses to make sure no detergent or salt residue remains in the glass as this can give strange flavours to wines and, in the case of sparkling wine, make it lose its sparkle more quickly. When polishing glasses it is best to use a linen cloth, as this will not leave bits of fluff in the glass.

Opening a Bottle of Still Wine
- Remove the top of the capsule, by cutting round below the lip of the bottle. This can be done with a capsule remover or knife.
- Wipe the neck of the bottle with a clean cloth.
- Draw the cork as gently and cleanly as possible using your selected corkscrew.
- Give the neck of the bottle a final clean inside and out.
- Pour a sample into the host's glass for approval.

Opening a Bottle of Sparkling Wine

It is important to remember that there is considerable pressure in a bottle of sparkling wine. Chilling to the correct temperature helps to reduce this. Even when the wine is chilled, it is possible for the cork to spring violently from the bottle and injure someone.

- Remove the foil and then the wire muzzle.
- The cork must be held in place by the hand from the moment the wire is removed.
- Tilt the bottle at an angle of about 30°, gripping the cork, and use the other hand to grip the base of the bottle.
- Turn the bottle, not the cork.
- Hold the cork steady, resisting its tendency to fly out, and ease it slowly out of the bottle.
- The gas pressure should be released with a quiet 'phut', not an explosion and flying cork.

Decanting Wine

Wines with a heavy deposit need to be decanted. This deposit is quite natural and is formed during the ageing process of many good red wines. Some young wines benefit from the aeration that occurs by being decanted, though this can be done as easily by swirling the wine in a glass. Note that 'airing' a wine by opening a bottle some time before service does ABSOLUTELY NO GOOD AT ALL. Too little of the wine is in contact with the air for it to have any effect.

- First remove the bottle horizontally from its rack and place in a decanting basket if available. Alternatively, hold carefully, making sure the deposit is not agitated.
- Very gently remove the top of the capsule and clean the shoulder and neck of the bottle. Very gently remove the cork.
- Remove the bottle from the basket, being careful not to disturb the deposit. Holding the bottle in front of a light, pour the wine carefully into the decanter until the deposit can be seen near the neck. At this point stop pouring.

ORDERING WINE

It is useful to know how many measures you can get from a standard 75cl bottle. This will help you work out how many bottles you would need for an order.

6 standard (small) 125ml glasses

4 generous 175ml glasses

3 large 250ml glasses

Appendix 2: Social Responsibility

Because of the harmful effects of excessive alcohol consumption, most countries have legislation to control its misuse. The legislation falls into four areas:
- minimum legal age to purchase or consume alcohol (LDA)
- maximum blood alcohol concentration (BAC) for drivers (and operators of other dangerous machinery)
- guidelines for sensible drinking
- restrictions covering the marketing, packaging and sale of alcohol.

These four elements are discussed in the following text, which has been supplied by AIM – Alcohol in Moderation. For further details about these topics, please consult the AIM website: www.alcoholinmoderation.com

There is relatively little international standardisation relating to alcohol legislation, and in some cases there are differences between states within a country. *For your examination, you are expected to know only about the laws that apply in the country where you are registered as a student.*

LEGAL AGE TO PURCHASE AND LEGAL DRINKING AGE (LDA)

In many countries a minimum age is set at which it becomes legal to drink or purchase alcohol. This drinking age provides a legally enforceable tool in preventing access to alcohol by those under a certain age on or off premises. Drinking age may be distinct from the minimum legal age at which a person may purchase alcohol. Most drinking-age legislation does not cover drinking in the home with parental permission and supervision. For example, this is legal from the age of 5 in the UK, while in many US states an underage person who drinks legally in a private residence is breaking the law if they step onto public property.

Drinking age (on premises) and purchasing age (off premises) is 18 for most countries, including Algeria, Argentina, Australia, Azerbaijan, Bahamas, Belarus, Belize, Bolivia, Botswana, Brazil, Bulgaria, Cape Verde, Central African Republic, Chile, China, Colombia, Congo, Republic of Costa Rica, Croatia, Czech Republic, Dominican Republic, Ecuador, El Salvador, Eritrea, Estonia, Ethiopia, Finland, Guatemala, Guyana, Hungary, Ireland, Israel, Kenya, Latvia, Lesotho, Lithuania, Malawi, Mauritius, Mexico, Mozambique, Namibia, New Zealand, Niger, Nigeria, Panama, Papua New Guinea, Peru, Philippines, Russia, Samoa, Seychelles, Singapore, Slovenia, South Africa, Sri Lanka, Taiwan, Trinidad and Tobago, Turkey, Turkmenistan, Uganda, Ukraine, Uruguay, Vanuatu, Venezuela, Zambia, Zimbabwe.

A few countries (Albania, Cambodia, Comoros, Equatorial Guinea, Gabon, Ghana, Guinea-Bissau, Kyrgyzstan, Togo) have no legislated limits on drinking age.

The exceptions are listed opposite.

Table 1: Drinking age variations

COUNTRY	DRINKING AGE ON PREMISES	PURCHASING AGE OFF PREMISES	NOTES
Albania	No limit	No limit	
Algeria	18	18	
Argentina	18	18	
Australia	18	18	
Austria	16/18 (see notes)	16/18 (see notes)	For spirits the age limit is 16 in three federal states and 18 in six federal states – 12% abv or higher may be consumed only at 18 and over in some states.
Azerbaijan	18	18	
Bahamas	18	18	
Belarus	18	18	
Belgium	16 beer and wine, 18 for spirits	None for beer and wine, 18 for spirits	
Belize	18	18	
Bolivia	18	18	
Botswana	18	18	
Brazil	18	18	
Brunei	Illegal	Illegal	
Bulgaria	18	18	
Burundi	16	16	
Cambodia	No limit	No limit	
Cameroon	18	21	
Canada	18/19 (see notes)	18/19 (see notes)	18 in Manitoba, Alberta and Quebec; 19 in all other provinces.
Cape Verde	18	18	
Central African Republic	18	18	
Chile	18	18	
China	18	18	
Colombia	18	18	
Comoros	No limit	No limit	
Congo	18	18	
Costa Rica, Republic of	18	18	
Croatia	18	18	
Cyprus	17	17	
Czech Republic	18	18	
Denmark	18	16	
Dominican Republic	18	18	
Ecuador	18	18	
Egypt	18 for beer, 21 for wine and spirits	18 for beer, 21 for wine and spirits	
El Salvador	18	18	
Equatorial Guinea	No limit	No limit	
Eritrea	18	18	
Estonia	18	18	
Ethiopia	18	18	
Fiji	21	21	
Finland	18	18	
France	16, but 18 for spirits	16, but 18 for spirits	
Gabon	No limit	No limit	

COUNTRY	DRINKING AGE ON PREMISES	PURCHASING AGE OFF PREMISES	NOTES
Gambia	Illegal (18 for non-Muslim population)	Illegal (18 for non-Muslim population)	
Georgia	16	16	
Germany	16 for beer and wine, 18 for spirits	16 for beer and wine, 18 for spirits	
Ghana	No limit	No limit	
Greece	17	None	
Guatemala	18	18	
Guinea-Bissau	No limit	No limit	
Guyana	18	18	
Hungary	18	18	
Iceland	20	20	
India	18 to 25, depending on state	18 to 25, depending on state	
Indonesia	21	21	
Ireland	18	18	
Israel	18	18	
Italy	16	16	
Jamaica	None	16	
Japan	20	20	
Kazakhstan	None	18	
Kenya	18	18	
Korea, Republic of (South Korea)	19	19	
Kyrgyzstan	No limit	No limit	
Latvia	18	18	
Lesotho	18	18	
Libya	Illegal	Illegal	
Lithuania	18	18	
Luxembourg	16	None	
Malawi	18	18	
Malta	16	16	
Mauritius	18	18	
Mexico	18	18	
Micronesia	21	21	
Morocco	None	16	
Mozambique	18	18	
Namibia	18	18	
Netherlands	16, but 18 for spirits above 15% abv	16, but 18 for spirits above 15% abv	
New Zealand	18	18	
Nicaragua	19	19	
Niger	18	18	
Nigeria	18	18	
Norway	18, but 20 for spirits above 22% abv	18, but 20 for spirits above 22% abv	
Pakistan	Illegal (21 for non-Muslim population)	Illegal (21 for non-Muslim population)	
Palau	21	21	
Panama	18	18	
Papua New Guinea	18	18	
Paraguay	20	20	

COUNTRY	DRINKING AGE ON PREMISES	PURCHASING AGE OFF PREMISES	NOTES
Peru	18	18	
Philippines	18	18	
Portugal	16	16	
Russia	18	18	
Samoa	18	18	
Seychelles	18	18	
Singapore	18	18	
Slovenia	18	18	
Solomon Islands	21	None	
South Africa	18	18	
Spain	18 (16 in Asturias)	18 (16 in Asturias)	
Sri Lanka	18	18	
Swaziland	None	18	
Sweden	18	20, but 18 for beer with 3.5% or less abv	
Switzerland	16/18 – depending on the canton – for beer and wine, 18 for spirits None	16/18 – depending on the canton – for beer and wine, 18 for spirits None	
Taiwan	18	18	
Togo	No limit	No limit	
Tonga	18	None	
Trinidad and Tobago	18	18	
Turkey	18	18	
Turkmenistan	18	18	
Uganda	18	18	
Ukraine	18	18	
United Kingdom	18 (see note)	18	Beer, wine and cider may be consumed on premises at 16 if with a table meal. (England and Wales: under-18s must be accompanied by an adult aged 18 or over.)
United States	21	21	Most states also ban underage people from having a BAC of 0.2 mg/ml in public, meaning that an underage person who drinks legally in a private residence is breaking the law if they step onto public property. Some states allow exceptions for educational, religious or medical purposes.
Uruguay	18	18	
Vanuatu	18	18	
Venezuela	18	18	
Zambia	18	18	
Zimbabwe	18	18	

BLOOD ALCOHOL CONCENTRATION (BAC) LIMITS

Defining BAC

A person's BAC level measures the amount of alcohol in the blood by recording the milligrams of ethanol per millilitre of blood. Most countries around the world have legal BAC limits for drivers, ranging from 0.0 mg/ml to 0.8 mg/ml, with different penalties applying for breaking the law. In some countries lower BAC limits are set for young, inexperienced drivers and/or for operators of commercial vehicles.

BAC levels are affected by how much alcohol has been drunk, and by the speed of drinking and over what period of time. An individual's weight, gender, health and food intake also affect the absorption and metabolism of alcohol, making an estimation of how much it is safe to drink before driving risky.

A person's risk of being involved in a traffic crash increases with the amount of alcohol consumed because their reactions slow down. Involvement in fatal crashes is 11 times more likely for drivers with BAC levels between 0.5 mg/ml and 0.9 mg/ml than for drivers who have not consumed alcohol, hence the recommendation to nominate a non-drinking 'designated driver' or to plan other ways of getting home safely when drinking.

Special legislation or BAC regulations are set nationally, at company level or internationally for operators of commercial vehicles, airline pilots and bus, truck and taxi drivers, as well as for captains of ships, for example. In some countries BAC limits apply to operators of bicycles, snowmobiles, personal aircraft and boats.

In most countries the standard BAC limit is 0.5 mg/ml:
Argentina, Australia, Austria, Belarus, Belgium, Bosnia and Herzegovina, Bulgaria, Cambodia, China, Denmark, El Salvador, Finland, France, Germany, Greece, Iceland, Israel, Italy, Kyrgyzstan, Macedonia, Mauritius, The Netherlands, Peru, Philippines, Portugal, Slovenia, South Africa, Spain, Switzerland, Thailand, Turkey, Uganda, Venezuela.

In many other counties, the limit is 0.8 mg/ml:
Botswana, Canada, Guatemala, Ireland, Kenya, Luxembourg, Malaysia, Malta, Mexico, New Zealand, Nicaragua, Paraguay, Singapore, United Kingdom, United States (federal law, though some states have lower limits, especially for drivers under 21), Uruguay, Zimbabwe.

A small number of countries have a limit of 0 mg/ml:
Armenia, Azerbaijan, Colombia, Croatia, Czech Republic, Ethiopia, Dominican Republic, Hungary, Nepal, Panama, Romania, Slovak Republic.

The exceptions are listed opposite.

Table 2: Standard BAC limits

COUNTRY	STANDARD BAC (IN MG/ML)
Albania	0.1
Algeria	0.1
Argentina	0.5
Armenia	0
Australia	0.5
Austria	0.5
Azerbaijan	0
Belarus	0.5
Belgium	0.5
Bolivia	0.7
Bosnia and Herzegovina	0.5
Botswana	0.8
Brazil	0.6
Bulgaria	0.5
Cambodia	0.5
Canada	0.8
China	0.5
Colombia	0
Costa Rica	0.49
Croatia	0
Czech Republic	0
Denmark	0.5
Dominican Republic	0
Ecuador	0.7
El Salvador	0.5
Ethiopia	0
Estonia	0.2
Finland	0.5
France	0.5
Georgia	0.3
Germany	0.5
Greece	0.5
Guatemala	0.8
Honduras	0.7
Hungary	0
Iceland	0.5
India	0.3
Ireland	0.8
Israel	0.5
Italy	0.5
Japan	0.3
Kenya	0.8
Kyrygyzstan	0.5

COUNTRY	STANDARD BAC (IN MG/ML)
Latvia	0.49
Lithuania	0.4
Luxembourg	0.8
Macedonia	0.5
Malaysia	0.8
Malta	0.8
Mauritius	0.5
Mexico	0.8
Moldova	0.3
Mongolia	0.2
Nepal	0
The Netherlands	0.5
New Zealand	0.8
Nicaragua	0.8
Norway	0.2
Panama	0
Paraguay	0.8
Peru	0.5
Philippines	0.5
Poland	0.2
Portugal	0.5
Romania	0
Russia	0.3
Singapore	0.8
Slovak Republic	0
Slovenia	0.5
South Africa	0.5
South Korea, Republic of	0.52
Spain	0.5
Sweden	0.2
Switzerland	0.5
Thailand	0.5
Turkey	0.5
Turkmenistan	0.3
Uganda	0.5
United Kingdom	0.8
United States (federal law; some states have lower limits, especially for drivers under 21)	0.8
Uruguay	0.8
Venezuela	0.5
Zimbabwe	0.8

SENSIBLE DRINKING GUIDELINES

Recommendations on drinking levels considered 'minimum risk' for men and women exist in many countries. Official guidelines on alcohol consumption are usually produced by government departments, public health bodies, medical associations or non-governmental organisations such as the World Health Organisation (WHO).

- Official drinking guidelines are issued by governments and public health entities to advise on levels of alcohol consumption considered 'safe', 'responsible' or 'low risk'. They do not apply to those under the legal drinking age or to pregnant women. Those on medication or with a history of illness should consult their GP for specific advice. Some guidelines suggest one or two alcohol-free days a week. Visit the websites cited for full country guidelines.

- Information included in guidelines offers recommendations on low-risk drinking levels for men and women, and may also define a standard drink or unit (which differ in each country) and offer advice to particular populations deemed to be at an increased risk of harm.

Standard drinks

Official 'drinks' or 'units' generally contain between 8 and 14 g of pure ethanol, although the measure varies among countries – there is no international consensus on a single standard drink size.

Means of tracking how much alcohol people are drinking can be a useful tool for those serving alcohol, as well as for those consuming it. In a number of countries, drinks are generally served in well-defined amounts at restaurants and bars. From a commercial perspective, this allows servers or retailers to monitor how much alcohol is being dispensed and ensures that drink sizes do not vary significantly across venues. For licensing authorities standard measures are a useful tool for tracking sales. The sizes of servings are largely shaped by local customs and cultures.

The strengths of different types of alcoholic beverage vary significantly, and using standard measures allows for uniformity. Thus, in terms of the alcohol it contains, a standard drink or unit will be the same – regardless of whether it contains beer, distilled spirits, wine or a mix of any of these beverages.

NB: Many countries have a maximum recommended gram intake per day without defining unit size – see below.

Table 3: International responsible drinking guidelines

COUNTRY	UNIT/STANDARD DRINK	RECOMMENDED GUIDELINES FOR ADULT LOW-RISK CONSUMPTION – MAXIMUM LEVELS IN GRAMS OF ALCOHOL
Argentina	N/A	Some information via: www.vivamosresponsablemente.com
Australia	10g	Men max. 4 drinks/day. Women 2 drinks/day 1 or 2 alcohol-free days every week. National Health and Medical Research Council (NHMRC): http://www.nhmrc.gov.au and Australian Department of Health and Ageing: http://www.alcohol.gov.au/ http://www.drinkwise.com.au/
Austria	10g	Men 24 g/day. Women 16 g/day Hazardous drinking: 60 g/day. Women 40 g/day Source: Federal Ministry for Labour, Health and Social Affairs: http://www.bmsg.gv.at
Belgium		No government guidelines
Canada	13.6g	Men 2 units/day. Women 2 units/day Men max. 14 units/week. Women max. 9 units/week Source: Centre for Addiction and Mental Health: http://www.camh.net and http://www.educalcool.qc.ca
Czech Republic	N/A	Men 24 g/day. Women 16 g/day National Institute of Public Health: www.szu.cz and http://www.forum-psr.cz/
Denmark	12g	Men 21 units/week. Women 14 units/week National Board of Health: www.sst.dk and http://www.goda.dk/
Finland	11g	Men 15 units/week. Women 10 units/week Alko Inc www.alko.fi
France	10g	Men 3 units/day. Women 2 units/day Based on WHO international guidelines cited by the Health Ministry, visit: www.2340.fr
Germany	10g	Men 3 units/day. Women 2 units/day No official government guidelines. Deutsche Weinakademie provides these recommendations. See www.drinkingandyou.com
Greece	10 g	Men 3 units/day. Women 2 units/day Ministry of Health
Hong Kong	Defined as 'a drink'	Men 3–4 units/day. Women 2–3 units/day Max. 21 units/week. Women max. 14 units/week Department of Health and Social Security
Hungary	N/A	Responsible drinking info via: http://www.hafrac.com
Iceland	N/A	Alcohol and Drug Abuse Prevention Council advises pregnant women to abstain when pregnant or if breast feeding
Indonesia	N/A	Ministry of Health national dietary guidelines state: 'avoid drinking alcoholic beverages'
Ireland	10 g	Men 21 units/week. Women 14 units/week www.drinkaware.ie
Italy	12 g	Men 2–3 units/day. Women 1–2 units/day Ministry of Health, more via: www.alcol.net
Japan	19.75 g	1–2 units/day (units larger than in other countries) Ministry of Health, Labour and Welfare
Luxembourg		Moderate consumption promoted without a precise definition
Malta	N/a	Responsible drinking guidelines via www.thesensegroup.org
Mexico		Responsible drinking advice via www.alcoholinformante.org.mex
Netherlands	10g	Men 4 units/day. Women 2 units/day www.stiva.nl and www.alcoholinfo.nl
New Zealand	10g	Men 3 units/day. Women 2 units/day Men max. 21 units/week. Women max. 14 units/week Alcohol Liquor Advisory Council: www.alcohol.org.nz
Norway	N/A	Visit www.alkokutt.no

COUNTRY	UNIT/STANDARD DRINK	RECOMMENDED GUIDELINES FOR ADULT LOW-RISK CONSUMPTION – MAXIMUM LEVELS IN GRAMS OF ALCOHOL
Poland	10g	Men 2 units/day. Women 1 unit/day 2 alcohol-free days a week recommended; PARPA: www.parpa.pl
Portugal	14 g (unofficial)	Men 2–3 units/day. Women 1–2 units/day National Council on Food and Nutrition
Romania	N/A	Men and women 32.5 g beer/day. Men and women 20.7 g wine/day Ministry of Health
Singapore	N/A	Ministry of Health National Dietary Guidelines state: 'limit alcohol intake to not more than 2 standard drinks a day (about 30 g alcohol)'.
Slovenia	N/A	Men 20 g/day. Women 10 g/day Men no more than max 50 g/day. Women 30 g on any one occasion Institute of Public Health
South Africa	N/A	Men max. 21 units/week. Women max. 14 units/week South African National Council on Alcoholism and Drug Dependence: http://www.ara.co.za/
Spain	10 g	Men max. 40g/day. Women max. 24g/day Ministry of Health national plan on drugs: www.alcoholysociedad.org
Sweden	N/A	Men max. 20g/day. Women max. 20g/day Swedish Research Council: www.vr.se
Switzerland	10–12 g	Men 2 units/day. Women max. 2 units/day Swiss Federal Commission for Alcohol Problems
Taiwan	N/A	Responsible drinking information via: www.tbaf.org.tw
Thailand	N/A	Ministry of Public Health states: 'avoid or reduce the consumption of alcoholic beverages'
United Arab Emirates	N/A	No official guidelines. Alcohol available in hotels to guests and visitors. Expatriate residents must possess a liquor permit, available to non-Muslims. Retail outlets sell only to permit holders for personal consumption. Providing alcohol to others is forbidden.
United Kingdom	8 g	Men 3–4 units/day. Women 2–3 units/day Men max. 21 units/week. Women max. 14 units/week Department of Health: http://www.units.nhs.uk and www.drinkingandyou.com
USA	14 g	Men up to 2 drinks/day. Women up to 1 drink/day Men max. 14 units/week. Women max. 7 units/week Department of Agriculture and Department of Health & Human Services www.healthierus.gov/dietaryguidelines and www.whatisadrink.com

NB: Some countries are not listed – where the consumption of alcohol is forbidden for religious reasons, for example.

For the many countries where there are no official government guidelines, such as Belgium, China, Germany, Hungary, India and Russia, it is recommended that the Internationally recognised World Health Organisation low-risk responsible drinking guidelines are followed. Taking a drink as 10 g, these are as follows:

(2)   Women should not drink more than 2 drinks a day on average

(3)   For men, not more than 3 drinks a day on average

(4)   Try not to exceed 4 drinks on any one occasion

(0)   Don't drink alcohol in specific situations such as when driving, if pregnant or in certain work situations, and abstain from drinking on at least one day a week.

Men or women who consistently drink more than the recommended levels may increase the risks to their health.

RESPONSIBLE ADVERTISING, MARKETING, PROMOTION, PRODUCTION, PACKAGING AND SALE OF ALCOHOL

As alcohol is harmful if drunk in excess, many laws, codes and guidelines exist to regulate and ensure that alcohol is produced, marketed and sold in a socially responsible manner. The monitoring of alcohol advertising, marketing, production and sales is addressed in a number of ways, particularly in relation to the protection of children and minors. There are voluntary codes developed by advertising self-regulatory organisations and social aspect organisations, and also individual company codes.

Many codes – such as the Portman Group code (UK), the Beer Institute and DISCUS Code (US) and MEAS (Ireland) – are reinforced with independent complaints panels, whereby the public may submit complaints concerning inappropriate advertising or marketing.

Provisions on naming, packaging and labelling are seen as one way to ensure that product development follows the same rules and high standards as those applicable to the marketing and advertising of drinks. Increasingly, responsible drinking messages are becoming standard on alcohol packaging, print and media internationally.

Watchdogs and regulatory frameworks, such as the EU Audio Visual Directive, largely lie above the self-regulatory codes. In some countries, such as Finland, the regulations are so strict that self-regulation is not necessary.

EU Law
Article 15 of the EU Audio Visual Directive states that the advertising of alcoholic beverages shall comply with the following criteria:

- it may not be aimed specifically at minors or, in particular, depict minors consuming these beverages;
- it shall not link the consumption of alcohol to enhanced physical performance or to driving;
- it shall not create the impression that the consumption of alcohol contributes towards social or sexual success;
- it shall not claim that alcohol has therapeutic qualities or that it is a stimulant, a sedative or a means of resolving personal conflicts, and it shall not encourage immoderate consumption of alcohol or present abstinence or moderation in a negative light;

- it shall not place emphasis on high-alcoholic content as being a positive quality of the beverages.

US Federal Law
In the USA at the federal level, beverage advertising is regulated by the Federal Alcohol Administration Act. The law forbids association with sports activities, such as the use of famous athletes consuming alcohol. The following are also forbidden:
- advertising aiming at the minor
- association with maturity
- use of high-alcohol degree as attractive
- suggesting that a beverage has therapeutical properties or that it enhances physical performance.

In addition to federal law, there are state laws and three self-regulation codes, one for each segment of the alcohol industry (beers, wines and spirits).

Most codes and guidelines from around the world embrace similar criteria. For a comprehensive list of codes and guidelines, visit the social and policy area of www.alcoholinmoderation.com

SENSIBLE DRINKING AND HEALTH

Are there any health benefits to moderate drinking?
With moderate drinking, as part of a healthy diet and lifestyle, the risk of developing cardiovascular disease and the risk of death from cardiovascular disease as well as all causes may be reduced by up to 30 per cent, especially for men over 40 and post-menopausal women for whom the risk factors for heart disease and strokes are highest. The risk increases exceptionally, however, with each drink above moderation. Drinking more than the guidelines (see above) will not provide more benefits, only more harm.

Statistically there are no health benefits for younger age groups who, for example, are at greater risk from alcohol-related violence and accidents. It is not recommended that anyone should start drinking for health reasons.

Alcohol may protect against cardiovascular disease because, in simple terms, it 'thins the blood' and so helps reduce the risk of harmful clots and clogging of the arteries. Small amounts of alcohol also stimulate the liver to produce 'good' cholesterol (HDL), which in turn carries off the harmful cholesterol (LDL) for disposal.

The message is little and often, however. Just one standard drink is enough to confer all the possible benefits, and the positive effect lasts for approximately 24 hours.

Several studies have confirmed that for middle-aged and older adults, very moderate drinking can confer health benefits, such as lowered risk of dementia, Alzheimer's disease, osteoporosis and Type 2 diabetes. Drinking more than 'moderately' can cause raised blood pressure and obesity, and can interfere with diabetes control, thus increasing the risk of both stroke and heart attacks.

When not to drink

Even mild intoxication can impair the ability to perform potentially dangerous tasks, such as driving a motor vehicle, operating machinery and working at heights. This is because alcohol slows down your reactions. As no safe threshold of consumption has been established during pregnancy, it is recommended that pregnant women and those planning to conceive should avoid alcohol. Alcohol does not mix with certain medications and a doctor's advice should be sought regarding alcohol consumption if medication is prescribed. Those with a history of mental illness or addiction should avoid alcohol.

ALCOHOL AND ITS METABOLISM

Alcohol is absorbed by the body through the stomach and small intestines. Food slows down the rate of absorption – that's why alcohol affects you more quickly on an empty stomach. Alcohol then enters the bloodstream and travels throughout the body, reaching the heart, brain, muscles and other tissues. This happens very quickly – within a few minutes. Usually, though not always, this has a pleasant effect.

The Role of the Liver

The body can't store alcohol, so it has to break it down – mostly via the liver. Through a complex metabolic process the liver first changes alcohol into acetaldehyde, a highly toxic substance. The acetaldehyde is converted by the liver into acetate, a harmless substance, which is then turned into carbon dioxide and water; these are then excreted from the body.

About 90–5 per cent of alcohol consumed is metabolised by the liver. The remaining 5–10 per cent is excreted through urine, breath and sweat. The body's ability to process alcohol depends on age, weight and sex, but on average the body breaks down alcohol at a rate of roughly one standard drink per hour. Hence drinking more than a drink an hour (taking a drink to be 8–10 g) will build up BAC and it may be many hours before a person is safe to drive. After a night of heavy drinking there is a risk of being over the drink-drive limit the next morning.

Size

A large, heavy person may not be affected by alcohol in the same way as a light, small person. This is because a larger person has more body fluids, which dilute the alcohol. Therefore the large, heavy person may have a lower BAC even when drinking the same amount at the same pace as a smaller person.

Recommended advice to keep blood alcohol levels down are to eat before starting to drink alcohol, and for consumers to pace themselves by not drinking too fast and to alternate each alcoholic drink with a soft drink. Also alcohol should preferably be enjoyed at meal times.

Gender

Women have proportionally less body water than men, so the concentration of alcohol in their blood streams is proportionately higher. There is also some evidence that women metabolise alcohol slightly differently. Women have smaller amounts of the enzyme ADH, which is responsible for breaking down alcohol in the liver and in the lining of the stomach and this may contribute to their higher blood alcohol levels.

Drinking too much, too fast

Alcohol is a mood-altering substance. It affects the nerves that pass messages around the body by slowing them down, and the more you drink the greater the effect. As you drink the alcohol passes into the bloodstream. Ethanol is the intoxicating part of alcohol and its molecules are so small that they can pass into the gaps between brain cells. Here they can interfere with the neurotransmitters (the brain's central post office) that govern all the brain's activities.

If you drink faster than one standard drink an hour, alcohol will start to flood the brain. Depending on how much and how fast you're drinking, this may affect the brain stem (even causing it to shut down) and that may in turn interfere with vital body functions. A young person, or somebody unused to drink, may experience this after just a few standard drinks taken at any one time.

Drinking to drunkenness

Getting drunk impairs your judgement and can increase risky behaviour, which could result in:
- an increased risk of sustaining injuries and being involved in accidents
- a greater risk of engaging in unsafe sex, which

could result in sexually transmitted infections and unplanned pregnancies
- an increased risk of being robbed or going home with a stranger
- an increased risk of fights, arguments and relationship problems
- an increased risk of gaining a criminal record
- in extreme cases, alcoholic poisoning, coma, brain damage and death.

Getting drunk or drinking heavily on a regular basis increases the risks of:
- alcohol dependence or alcoholism
- sexual difficulties, including impotence
- cirrhosis of the liver and alcoholic fatty liver
- cardiac arrest and stroke
- pancreatitis
- stomach disorders, such as ulcers
- certain types of cancer, especially of the aero-digestive tract and breast cancer.

It is important to remember that 'the majority of people who drink alcohol drink sensibly the majority of the time'. Also, more than half of the world's adult population chooses not to drink alcohol for religious, cultural or health reasons.

For a balanced perspective and more detail about current research into the effects of alcohol on health, we recommend you consult the Alcohol in Moderation (AIM) websites:
www.drinkingandyou.com
and
www.alcoholinmoderation.com

Glossary

Abbreviations **F** = French **G** = German **I** = Italian **P** = Portuguese **S** = Spanish
r = region **w** = white grape variety **b** = black grape variety

The main text contains everything you will need to know to pass the WSET Intermediate Certificate Exam. This Glossary is included as a reference resource to cover a number of other labels and production terms that are not part of the WSET Intermediate Certificate syllabus, but which you may encounter from time to time.

Abboccato	**I**	Medium-sweet and full-bodied.
Acetic acid		The acid component of vinegar present in small quantities in all wines. Excessive amounts result in a vinegary nose and taste.
Adamado	**P**	Sweet.
Adega	**P**	Winery.
Agiorgitiko	**b**	Greek black variety (used in Nemea). Low in acidity, with soft tannins and rich, plummy fruit.
Aglianico	**b**	High quality black variety from southern Italy. High tannin and acid, complex fruit and good ageability. Used for Taurasi and Aglianico del Vulture.
Albariño	**w**	Fruity high-acid dry white from northwest Spain. Main region is Rías Baixas DO.
Alcohol		Potable alcohol, as contained in alcoholic drinks, is ethanol, sometimes called ethyl alcohol. Actual alcohol is the amount of ethanol present in a wine, measured as a percentage of the total volume at 20° C as shown on the label.
Aligoté	**w**	High-acid inexpensive dry white from Burgundy, usually unoaked. Will be varietally labelled to distinguish these wines from Chardonnay.
Almacenista	**S**	A producer of Sherry who ages it and then sells it in bulk to a merchant.
Alte Reben	**G**	Old vines.
Amabile	**I**	Medium-sweet.
Anbaugebiet	**G**	Designated quality wine region.
Annata	**I**	Vintage.
Aragonez	**b**	Tempranillo (in Portugal), also called Tinta Roriz.
Assemblage	**F**	Blending of a number of different parcels of wine, particularly in Bordeaux or Champagne.
Assyrtiko	**w**	White variety with pronounced fruit and high acidity; the wines are usually dry and unoaked. From Greece, particularly Santorini. (Some sweet versions are also made, from dried grapes).
Ausbruch	**G**	An Austrian quality category for sweet wines; the minimum must weight required is higher than that for *Beerenauslese*, but lower than that for *Trockenbeerenauslese*.
Azienda (or casa)	**I**	An estate that makes wine from both its own and bought-in grapes.
Azienda (or casa) agricola	**I**	An estate that uses only its own grapes in the production of its wine.
Azienda (or casa) vinicola	**I**	A producer who buys in and vinifies grapes.
Baga	**b**	High-acid, high-tannin Portuguese black grape, usually oak-aged. The main region is Bairrada.
Bandol	**r**	AC Region in Provence, mainly making long-lived, full-bodied red wines from Mourvèdre (q.v.).
Bardolino	**r**	Red wine DOC region in northeast Italy; wines are similar in style to Valpolicella DOC.
Barrique	**F**	Cask (q.v.) with a capacity of 225 litres. Traditional to Bordeaux, but now used throughout the world.
Barsac	**r**	AC Region neighbouring Sauternes, making wines of a similar style, quality and price.
Bereich	**G**	A group of communes (*Gemeinde*).
Bergerac	**r**	AC Region inland of Bordeaux, making wines in a similar style (red and white).
Bin		Literally a location, for example in a cellar, where a particular wine is stored. Often used as part of a brand name.
Biologique	**F**	Organic.
Blaufränkisch	**b**	Red cherry fruit and peppery spice. Oaked/unoaked. Austria (especially Burgenland) plus Germany and Hungary.
Blended whisk(e)y		Scotland: a blend of grain and malt whisky. USA: A blend of straight whiskey and neutral corn spirit.
Bodega	**S**	Winery.
Bonnezeaux	**r**	Loire AC region making sweet wines from noble-rot affected Chenin Blanc grapes.
Borderies	**r**	A region in Cognac, just north of Grande and Petite Champagne (q.v.), offering very high quality spirits.

Botanicals		Flavourings used in gin production, such as juniper, coriander and citrus peel.
Botrytis cinerea		Fungus which attacks the grape berry. In certain circumstances it will form unwanted grey rot; in others, desirable noble rot.
Bottiglia	I	Bottle.
Brunello di Montalcino	r	Region in Tuscany making Chianti-style red wines from Sangiovese.
Brut	F, S	Dry (of a sparkling wine).
Bull's Blood		Medium-bodied Hungarian red made from a blend of varieties, including Blaufränkisch and international varieties.
Bush vines		Vines trained as free-standing plants, not needing the support of a trellis.
Butt		Traditional barrel used in Sherry production, holding about 600 litres.
Cabernet Franc	b	Black variety similar to Cabernet Sauvignon, but with softer tannins and more vegetal flavours important in Bordeaux (especially Saint Emilion).
Cahors	r	AC region in southwest France, making full-bodied reds, mainly from Malbec.
Calvados	r	Delimited region in northwest France, making apple (and pear)-based aged spirits.
Cantina sociale	I	Co-operative cellar.
Cap Classique		A South African sparkling wine made using the traditional method (see Chapter 22).
Carbonic maceration		Fermentation of whole bunches of black grapes with the berries initially intact. The intracellular fermentation results in well-coloured, fruity red wines, with little tannin.
Carignan	b	High-acid, high-tannin black variety. Suits hot regions such as the south of France and North Africa.
Cascina	I	Farmhouse (has come to mean estate).
Cask		Wooden barrel, usually made of oak, used for fermentation, maturation and storage of wines. Traditional names and sizes vary from region to region.
Cask strength		Particularly of Malt Whiskies, a spirit that has not been reduced (watered down) to a bottling strength of around 40% abv. These generally will not be filtered and will be very high in alcohol: sometimes over 75% abv. See also overproof.
Casta	P	Grape variety.
Cave	F	Cellar (often underground) or winemaking establishment.
Cave coopérative	F	Co-operative cellar.

Cépage	F	Grape variety.
Cerasuolo	I	Cherry pink.
Chai	F	Above-ground warehouse for storing wine, usually in barrels.
Chambolle-Musigny	r	Commune AC in the Côte de Nuits famous for Pinot Noir.
Chaptalisation		Must enrichment (adding sugar to the grape juice to increase potential alcohol) specifically using beet or cane, named after Comte Chaptal, the Napoleonic minister who advocated its use.
Château	F	Vineyard in Bordeaux, generally, but not always, with accompanying house.
Chaume	r	Loire AC region making sweet wines from noble-rot affected Chenin Blanc. The best part of this is Quarts de Chaume AC.
Chiaretto	I	Light or pale rosé.
Cinsault	b	Black variety with savoury, meaty flavours. Suits hot conditions such as the southern Rhône (where it is blended with Grenache, Syrah and Mourvèdre) and South Africa.
Climat	F	A vineyard site.
Clos	F	Historically, a walled vineyard, though the walls may no longer exist.
Colombard	w	White variety grown in southwest France for distillation, and for high-acid, appley dry whites.
Commune		A small wine-growing region, usually surrounding one village.
Condrieu	r	Northern Rhône AC region making complex, expensive, exotic dry and off-dry whites from Viognier (q.v.).
Consorzio	I	Producers' trade association, whose members' wines are identified by an individually designed neck-label.
Continentality		The difference between summer and winter temperatures.
Co-operative cellar		Winemaking (and sometimes bottling and marking) facilities that are jointly owned by a number of growers.
Cornas	r	Northern Rhône AC region making full-bodied reds from Syrah.
Cortese	w	Variety used in Northern Italy (especially Gavi) for high-acid, unoaked dry whites with green and citrus fruit (pear, lemon).
Corton	r	Grand Cru AC in the Côte de Beaune, making red (Pinot Noir) and white (Chardonnay) wines. Includes Corton-Charlemagne Grand Cru AC.
Corvina	b	The main variety used (along with Molinara and Rondinella) for Valpolicella. High-acid, medium tannin, and cherry and prune fruit.

Côte	F	Hillside.
Côte Chalonnaise	r	Burgundy district making wines with some of the style and quality of those from the Côte d'Or, but at lower prices. See also Mercurey, Givry, Rully, Montagny.
Coteau(x)	F	Slope(s).
Coteaux du Layon	r	Loire AC region making sweet wines from noble-rot affected Chenin Blanc grapes.
Cru	F	A single 'growth', generally of quality. It might be a village or a vineyard.
Cru Artisan	F	A rank of Bordeaux châteaux, below *Cru Bourgeois* (q.v.).
Cru Bourgeois	F	A rank of Bordeaux châteaux, below *Cru Classé* (q.v.).
Cru Classé	F	A classified growth, normally in Bordeaux.
Cuvée	F	A blend, which could be of different varieties, regions or vintages, or it could be of different barrels or vats from the same estate or vineyard.
Dégorgement	F	See disgorgement (q.v.).
Dégorgement tardive	F	A Champagne that has been disgorged after an exceptionally long period of yeast autolysis.
Demi-sec	F	Medium-dry.
Disgorgement		Removal of the sediment from a bottle in traditional method sparkling wine production (*dégorgement*).
Dolcetto	b	Piemontese black variety with juicy black fruit, soft tannins and moderate acidity.
Domaine	F	Estate.
Dosage	F	Adjustment of the sugar level in sparkling wines by the addition of *liqueur d'expedition* (q.v.) after disgorgement (q.v.).
Eau-de-vie	F	Spirit distilled to a maximum of 96% abv: literally, 'water of life'.
Edelfaule	G	Noble rot.
Edes (Hungary)		Sweet.
Einzellage	G	Individual vineyard.
Elaborado (por)	S	Produced (by).
Elevé en fûts de chêne	F	Aged in oak barrels.
Embotellado (por)	S	Bottled (by).
En Primeur	F	Wines, especially from Bordeaux, that are sold before they are bottled.
Entre-Deux-Mers	r	AC Region in Bordeaux making dry whites.

Erzeugerabfullung	G	Bottled by the producer.
Estate		A producer who makes wine from grapes grown on their property only.
Ethanol		See alcohol.
Extra-sec	F	Off-dry (sparkling wines).
Fattoria	I	Estate.
Federspiel	G	In the Wachau, a category lying in between Steinfeder and Smaragd (q.v.).
Fine Champagne	r	On a bottle of Cognac, indicates that the grapes used come exclusively from Grande Champagne and Petite Champagne (q.v.), with the majority coming from Grande Champagne.
Fining		Removal of matter in suspension in a wine by the addition of a fining agent such as bentonite, which acts as a coagulant. Occasionally animal products are used, making such wines unsuitable for vegetarians, although none of the fining agent remains in the wine.
Flor	S	Yeast growth which forms particularly on the surface of Fino and Manzanilla Sherries, giving them a distinctive taste and protecting them from oxidation.
Frizzante	I	Slightly sparkling.
Garganega	w	The dominant variety in the highest-quality Soave wines. Green fruit, crisp acidity, medium-body.
Garrafeira	P	A superior wine with additional ageing.
Gavi (di Gavi)	r	DOCG region in Piemonte, making high-acid dry white wines from Cortese (q.v.).
Gigondas	r	Southern Rhône AC region making Grenache-dominated wines, comparable in style and quality to Châteauneuf-du-Pape.
Givry	r	AC Commune in the Côte Chalonnaise, making red (Pinot Noir) and White (Chardonnay) wines.
Grains nobles (sélection de...)	F	Botrytis-affected grapes (wine made using a selection of nobly rotten grapes). This is a legal description in Alsace, but the phrase may occasionally be seen on wines from other regions, such as Condrieu, Mâcon and Côteaux du Layon.
Grande Champagne	r	The quality centre of the Cognac region; a source of particularly elegant, complex spirits that age well in oak. See also Petit Champagne, Fine Champagne, Borderies.
Granvas	S	Tank-fermented sparkling wine.
Grechetto	w	Medium to high acid white variety that is used for the best Orvieto DOC wines. Suitable for dry and medium (amabile) styles.
Grenache Blanc	w	White-skinned version of Grenache, used in southern France and northern Spain for full-bodied peachy whites with medium to low acidity.

Grosslage	**G**	A group of adjoining vineyards. Not to be confused with *Einzellage*.
Grüner Veltliner	**w**	High-quality grape variety grown in Austria. Styles range from light-bodied and refreshing to powerful and complex.
Highland	**r**	Scottish region, north of a line from Greenock to Dundee. Malt Whiskies from this region are generally very intensely flavoured. See also Islay, Speyside, Lowland.
Imbottigliato all'origine	**I**	Estate-bottled.
Invecchiato	**I**	Aged.
Islay	**r**	Island off the west coast of Scotland. Islay Malt Whiskies are generally very peaty, with seaweed, medicinal and brine aromas. See also Highland, Speyside, Lowland.
Jumilla	**r**	Hot region in southeast Spain, making dark-coloured, full-bodied reds mainly from Monastrell (Mourvèdre).
Lambrusco	**b**	Traditionally a fruity, dry (or off-dry) sparkling red from Italy, made from the Lambrusco grape variety. Much exported Lambrusco is a sweet, lightly-sparkling white that is light in alcohol.
Lees		The sediment of dead yeast cells that gathers at the bottom of the tank or cask once fermentation is completed.
Lees stirring		A process of mixing the lees (q.v.) with the wine, usually in cask, to help extract components that will give the wine extra flavour and body.
Lieu Dit	**F**	A named vineyard site not of *Premier Cru* or *Grand Cru* status.
Liqueur d'expédition	**F**	A liquid mixture of wine and sugar, added to all bottle-fermented sparkling wines after disgorgement and before final corking. See dosage (q.v.).
Liqueur de tirage	**F**	Mixture of wine, sugar and yeast added to still wine to promote a secondary fermentation in sparkling wine production.
Liquoreux	**F**	Very sweet, especially botrytis-affected wines.
Liquoroso	**I**	Strong, often fortified, wine.
Lowland	**r**	Scottish region, south of the line from Greenock to Dundee. Lowland Malt Whiskies are generally light and smooth, with floral, grassy and cereal aromas. See also Highland, Islay, Speyside.
Maceration		Period of time when the skins are in contact with the juice or wine during red wine vinification.
Madeira	**r**	Aged, fortified wine from the island of Madeira. Comes in dry, medium and sweet styles. Grape varieties are named on premium and vintage versions: Sercial (dry), Verdelho (off-dry), Boal (Sweet), Malmsey (very sweet).
Madiran	**r**	AC region in southwest France, making full-bodied reds, mainly from Tannat (q.v.).
Malolactic fermentation		Conversion of harsh malic acid into softer lactic acid by the action of lactic bacteria. As a side effect, buttery, nutty flavour compounds can be produced.
Malt		Barley which has undergone the malting process of soaking, germination and kilning to convert the starch present in the original grain into fermentable sugar.
Malvasia	**w**	Fruity, aromatic grape variety used for the sweetest Madeiras (Malmsey), and some non-fortified sweet wines. Also used for the finest Frascati and White Rioja though Trebbiano and Viura are more common.
Manipulant	**F**	A grape-grower who also makes wine, especially in Champagne.
Marc	**F**	1. The residue of skins, pips and stalks left in a press after the extraction of juice or wine. In English, this is called pomace. 2. Brandy made from this, rather than whole grapes.
Marsanne	**w**	Delicately-flavoured, low-acid grape variety used for many full-bodied dry white Rhône wines, including white Hermitage AC. Often blended with Roussanne.
Mas	**F**	Vineyard.
Maso, Masseria	**I**	Estate.
Mataro	**b**	Mourvèdre (q.v.), especially in Australia.
Menetou-Salon	**r**	Loire AC region making Sancerre-style white wines from Sauvignon Blanc, and some light reds from Pinot Noir.
Merchant		1. A company that buys grapes or finished wine for vinification, maturation and blending before sale. 2. A wine dealer.
Mercurey	**r**	Region in the Côte Chalonnaise, best known for reds (Pinot Noir).
Metodo charmat	**I**	Tank method sparkling wine.
Metodo classico, Metodo tradizionale	**I**	Traditional method, bottle-fermented sparkling wine.
Mezcal		General category for Agave-based spirits. Tequila is a Mezcal from a delimited region.
Micro-climate		The climate within the canopy of the vine.
Millésimé	**F**	Vintage date.
Mise en bouteille (par)	**F**	Bottled (by).

Mise en bouteille au château/domaine	**F**	Château/domain-bottled.
Mise sur lie	**F**	Bottled directly from the lees (q.v.).
Mistelle, mistela	**F, S**	A mixture of unfermented grape juice and alcohol, such as Pineau de Charentes, Ratafia and most Moscatel de Valencia.
Moelleux	**F**	Medium-sweet.
Monastrell	**b**	Mourvèdre (q.v), especially in Spain.
Monbazillac	**r**	Appellation within the Bergerac region (q.v.) making Sauternes-style sweet wines, mainly from Sémillon.
Monopole	**F**	A vineyard, especially in Burgundy, that has only one owner.
Montagny	**r**	Côte Chalonnaise region making white wines from Chardonnay.
Morey-Saint-Denis	**r**	AC Commune in the Côte de Nuits, best known for red (Pinot Noir).
Mourvèdre	**b**	Hot-climate variety making deep-coloured, high-tannin full-bodied spicy reds. Appears as part of the blend in southern Rhône, and alone in Bandol.
Mousseux	**F**	Sparkling.
Muffa nobile	**I**	Noble rot.
Must		Unfermented grape juice, destined to become wine.
Naoussa	**r**	Region in northern Greece making high-acid, high-tannin reds from Xinomavro.
Négociant	**F**	Merchant (q.v.).
Negroamaro	**b**	Southern Italian black variety. Literally 'black-bitter'. Used in Salice Salentino.
Nemea	**r**	Greek region making full-bodied soft fruity reds from Agiorgitiko.
Nero d'Avola	**b**	Sicilian black grape variety, used for full-bodied reds.
Non-filtré	**F**	Unfiltered.
Overproof		Most commonly used of Rum. Any spirit that is higher in alcohol than proof spirit (q.v.).
Palo Cortado		Dry style of Sherry that has similar flavours to Amontillado, but is more full-bodied.
Passito	**I**	A generally strong, sweet wine made from partially dried grapes.
Pétillant	**F**	Lightly sparkling.
Petit château	**F**	In Bordeaux, one of the many château brands that fall outside the classifications.

Petite Champagne	**r**	The Cognac region surrounding Grande Champagne (q.v.). Spirits made from Petite Champagne grapes are very high quality, but not quite as elegant, complex and ageworthy as those from Grande Champagne. See also Fine Champagne.
Pinot Blanc/ Pinot Bianco	**w**	White variety grown in Alsace and Northern Italy. Similar in flavour to Chardonnay, but usually unoaked or very lightly oaked.
Pipe		Traditional cask (q.v.) used in the Douro for Port production. Two sizes are recognised: the 550-litre production, or Douro, pipe and the 534-litre shipping pipe.
Podere	**I**	A small estate.
Pourriture noble	**F**	Noble rot.
Prädikat	**G**	The various subcategories of German Quality wines (*Kabinett, Spätlese, Auslese, Beerenauslese, Trockenbeerenauslese,* as well as *Eiswein*). Austria adds the category *Ausbruch,* but does not include *Kabinett*.
Primary aromas		Aromas in a wine that arise directly from the fruit (q.v. secondary, tertiary).
Priorat/Priorato	**r**	DOC region in Catalunya, making intensely-flavoured full bodied reds from old-vine Grenache and varieties.
Produttore	**I**	Producer.
Proof		Of spirits, 57.1% abv (UK), 50% abv (USA). See also overproof.
Propriétaire	**F**	Owner.
Pupitre	**F**	Rack consisting of two hinged boards through which holes have been bored to hold the necks of sparkling wine bottles during riddling (q.v.).
Puttunyos		Measure of sweetness in a Tokaji wine.
Quinta	**P**	Farm or estate.
Racking		Drawing off clear wine from a cask or vat and moving it to another, leaving the sediment behind.
Raisin	**F**	Grape.
Recioto	**I**	Similar to passito (q.v.), made with part-dried grapes.
Récoltant	**F**	Someone who harvests their own grapes.
Remuage	**F**	Riddling (q.v.).
Reserve		May indicate a superior quality wine, or wines that have seen a period of ageing. Or it may indicate very little. Unlike the word *Reserva* or *Riserva* in Spain, Portugal or Italy, this word has no legal meaning.
Residual sugar		Unfermented sugar remaining in the wine after bottling. Even dry wines will contain a small amount.

Reuilly	r	AC Loire region making Sancerre-style white wines from Sauvignon Blanc, and some light reds from Pinot Noir.
Rìas Baixas	r	DO Region in northwest Spain, making crisp, fruity dry white wines from Albariño.
Ribatejo	r	Portuguese region, making red and white wines.
Rich	F	Sweet (sparkling wines).
Riddling		Moving the sediment to the neck of the bottle before disgorgement (q.v.) in traditional method sparkling wine production.
Roussanne	w	High quality white Rhône variety. Usually blended (with Marsanne in the northern Rhône; with other varieties in the south). Full-bodied, medium to high acidity, orchard fruit flavours.
Ruby Cabernet	b	NOT Cabernet Sauvignon (though it is related). A variety created especially for very hot conditions such as Central Valley, California. Mainly used for simple, soft, fruity reds.
Rueda	r	DO region west of Ribera del Duero, making crisp, unoaked, fruity dry white wines from Verdejo and Sauvignon Blanc.
Rully	r	Côte Chalonnaise (q.v.) region, best known for white wines (Chardonnay) and Sparkling wines.
Sainte-Croix-du-Mont	r	Region facing Sauternes across the River Garonne, making wines in a similar style but at lower prices.
Saint-Estèphe	r	Commune in the Haut-Médoc.
Saint-Joseph	r	Region in the northern Rhône, mainly making red wines from Syrah.
Saint-Julien	r	Commune in the Haut-Médoc.
Salice Salentino	r	DOC Region in southern Italy, making full-bodied red wines mainly from Negroamaro (q.v.).
Savennières	r	AC region in the Loire, making complex, long-lived dry white wines from Chenin Blanc.
Secondary aromas		Aromas in a wine that arise from the fermentation (q.v. primary, tertiary aromas).
Single cask		Particularly of Malt Whiskies, a spirit that is not a blend of several casks. These are often bottled unfiltered, at cask strength (q.v.).
Site climate		The climate of a plot of vines, perhaps a vineyard, or part of a vineyard.
Smaragd	G	In the Wachau (Austria), rich, full-bodied dry wines from late-harvested grapes.
Solera		System of fractional blending used in the production of Sherry, wherein older wine is refreshed by the addition of younger wine.
Speyside	r	Scottish region, within the Highlands (q.v.). Speyside Malt Whiskies are generally very elegant, and well-balanced, with subtle peat and complex fruit, floral and honey aromas. See also Islay, Lowland.
Spumante	I	Sparkling wine made by any method.
Steinfeder	G	In the Wachau (Austria), the lightest bodied wine category for dry wines.
Straight whiskey		USA. A whiskey made from at least 51 per cent of one grain, distilled to no more than 80% abv, and aged for a minimum of two years in new oak casks.
Strohwein, Schilfwein	G	Sweet wine made from grapes that have been dried on straw or reed mats.
Sulphur dioxide (SO₂)		Highly reactive and pungent gas which is used in winemaking as an anti-oxidant and antiseptic (additive E220).
Supérieur	F	Indicates a higher degree of alcohol.
Super Second		Bordeaux châteaux that were second (or third) growths in the 1855 Classification, but which sometimes produce wines that rival the first growths for quality. Which châteaux qualify is a matter of debate.
Sur pointe	F	Ageing of a bottle of sparkling wine, neck down, after yeast autolysis is complete, but before disgorgement.
Szamorodni (Hungary)		'As it comes'. Wine made from grapes that have not been sorted according to their degree of botrytis.
Száraz (Hungary)		Dry.
Tannat	b	High-tannin black grape variety grown in southwest France (especially Madiran AC), also popular in Uruguay. Often blended with Merlot.
Tarrango	b	Grape variety developed for hot conditions, used for light-bodied, Beaujolais-style reds, mainly in Australia.
Tavel	r	Southern Rhône AC specialising in full-bodied dry Grenache-based rosés.
Tenuta	I	Estate.
Terroir	F	A sense of place expressed in a wine, which may include the effects of climate, site climate, soils, aspect, slope, and even local grape varieties, yeast cultures and winemaking practices.
Tertiary aromas		Aromas in a wine that are due to the effects of ageing (q.v. primary, secondary aromas).
Toro	r	DO region in Spain, neighbouring Rueda (q.v.), making intensely fruity red wines, mainly from Tempranillo.
Touriga Nacional	b	Portugal's most prestigious black grape variety. Part of the blend for the best Ports. Also used for complex, long-lived full-bodied dry reds with high tannin levels.
Tri (pl. Tries)	F	A selection of grapes, especially those grapes picked during one passage through a vineyard, selected at the perfect level of ripeness for sweet wines.

Trincadeira	**b**	Portuguese black variety, used for soft, plummy reds.
Uva	**I**	Grape.
Uvaggio	**I**	Blend of grapes.
Vacqueras	**r**	Southern Rhône AC region, making wines comparible in quality and style to Châteauneuf-du-Pape.
Vecchio	**I**	Old. For DOC wines there are controls as to how this word may be used.
Vendange	**F**	The wine harvest.
Vendange à la main	**F**	Hand-harvested.
Vendange Tardive, VT	**F**	Late-harvest. A wine made with exceptionally ripe grapes.
Verdejo	**w**	High quality white fruity-aromatic grape variety, used for unoaked dry whites in Rueda (q.v.).
Verdelho	**w**	White grape variety used for fortified wines (especially in Madeira), for fruity dry whites.
Verdicchio	**w**	High-acid white grape variety grown in the Marche (especially Verdiccio dei Castelli di Jesi).
Vernaccia	**w**	High-acid white grape variety grown in Tuscany (especially Vernaccia di San Gimignano).
Vieilles vignes	**F**	Old vines. Not a legally defined term. Old vines give lower yields of generally higher quality grapes.
Viejo	**S**	Old.
Vigna, vigneto	**I**	Vineyard.
Vignoble	**F**	Vineyard.
Viña	**S**	Vineyard.
Vin de paille	**F**	Wine made from grapes that have been dried.
Vine/grape variety		One of a number of recognisable members of a particular vine species. They may result from natural mutation or deliberate crossing.
Vine species		Any of the members of the genus *Vitis*. Most wine is made from European species, *Vitis vinifera*, but using American rootstocks from the species *V. rupestris* or *V. riparia*.
Vinha	**P**	A plot of vines.
Vinification		Winemaking.
Vino generoso	**S**	Fortified wine.
Vino Nobile di Montepulciano	**r**	Region in Tuscany making Chianti-style red wines from Sangiovese.

Vino novello	**I**	New wine, bottled shortly after the harvest.
Viognier	**w**	High quality white grape variety, originally from the northern Rhône (Condrieu). Now grown more widely in southern France and New World countries. Gives exotically-scented (nashi-pear, white peach, violet, minerals), full-bodied, dry and off-dry wines.
Viticoltore, vigniaiolo	**I**	Grower.
Viticulture		Grape growing.
Vitigno	**I**	Grape variety.
Viura	**w**	Spanish white variety, used for white Rioja and (Along with Parellada and Xarel-lo) Cava. Also known as Maccabeo.
Vivace	**I**	'Lively'. Slightly sparkling.
Volatile acidity		Acetic acid (q.v.) in a wine. A small amount exists in all wines and is an important part of the aroma or bouquet. Excessive amounts indicate a faulty wine.
Volnay	**r**	AC Commune in the Côte de Beaune, specialising in red wines (Pinot Noir).
VOS, VORS		*Vinum Optimum Signatum*, *Vinum Optimum Rare Signatum*. These are age classifications for very old Sherries. VOS indicates an average age of at least 20 years; VORS indicates an average age of at least 30 years.
Vosne-Romanée	**r**	AC Commune in the Côte de Nuits, specialising in red wines (Pinot Noir). Includes Romanée-Conti Grand Cru AC.
Vougeot	**r**	AC Commune in the Côte de Nuits, specialising in red wines (Pinot Noir). Includes Clos de Vougeot Grand Cru.
Winzergenossenschaft	**G**	Co-operative cellar.
Xinomavro	**b**	High-acid, high-tannin Greek grape variety (sometimes compared to Nebbiolo). Used in several Northern Greek regions, including Naoussa.
Yeast		Generic term for a number of single-celled micro-organisms which produce zymase, the enzyme responsible for converting sugar into alcohol. The most important wine yeast is *Saccharomyces cerevisiae*.
Yeast autolysis		Breakdown of dead yeast cells after the secondary fermentation in sparkling wine production. Among other things, it gives the wine a yeasty, or biscuity, nose.
Yecla	**r**	Hot DO region in southeast Spain, making dark-coloured, full-bodied reds mainly from Monastrell (Mourvedre).

Index

Numbers in **bold** type indicate significant references.